THE WAY TO PUNCTUATE

THE WAY TO PUNCTUATE

WILLIAM D. DRAKE

State University of New York at Oswego

CHANDLER PUBLISHING COMPANY
An Intext Publisher • Scranton / London / Toronto

Copyright © 1971 by Chandler Publishing Company
All rights reserved
International Standard Book Number 0-8102-0388-x
Library of Congress Catalog Number 79-123580
Printed in the United States of America

CONTENTS

How to Use This Book — ix

PART I. Punctuating Standard Prose Sentences — 1

1. Place a comma after each item in a series — 2
2. How to avoid three common errors in punctuating a series — 5
3. Do not separate two coordinate words or phrases with a comma — 6
4. How to place commas in a string of modifiers — 8
5. How to place commas in a series of word groups — 10
6. Use semicolons to separate items in more complicated series — 12
7. Use a comma between sentences connected by **and, but, or, nor,** or **yet** — 14
8. Do not connect sentences with a comma alone — 17
9. A semicolon may be used between sentences in place of a comma — 19
10. A semicolon may also substitute for a conjunction — 20
11. Place a comma after an introductory or transitional expression — 20
12. Place a pair of commas around a transitional expression when it is moved further on into the sentence — 21
13. Do not mistake a transitional word for a conjunction — 22
14. How to use commas with other movable phrases — 26

v

15. How to use commas with movable clauses   30
16. How to use commas with other sentence elements out of normal order   32
17. How to use commas with adjective clauses   34
18. How to use commas with appositives   37
19. How to use commas with verbal phrases   39
20. How to use commas with interruptive words or word groups   43
21. How to use pairs of dashes   46
22. How to use parentheses   47
23. How to use the single dash   51
24. How to use the colon   55
25. How to end a sentence   58
26. How to quote from another author's work   61
    Quoting an entire sentence or paragraph :: Introducing a quotation :: Indirect quotations :: Incorporating quoted material into a sentence :: Breaking a quotation into two parts :: Inserting a break between two quoted sentences :: Indicating the omission of words from a quotation :: Inserting editorial comment within a quotation :: Quoting within a quotation :: Quoting titles :: Quoting lines of poetry
27. Other uses (and abuses) of quotation marks   71
28. Putting it all together   73
    Showing omissions :: Pointing up contrast :: Showing a restatement or enlargement for clarity

PART II. Arbitrary Marks and Usages   83

29. The hyphen separates parts of words   83
    Division of a word at the end of a line :: Separate individual letters with a hyphen to indicate spelling :: Separate individual letters to indicate stuttering

30. The hyphen joins the parts of some compound words   86
   Noun compounds derived from a verb and ending in **-er** or **-ing** :: Compounds derived from a verb and adverb :: Compound adjectives derived from participles :: Compound adjectives in which the two elements retain independent meaning :: Compound verbs derived from a verb and a phrase, or verb and adverb :: Phrases used as compound nouns or adjectives :: Suspended compounds :: Hyphenation for clarification

31. The hyphen sometimes separates the prefix from a base word   91
   Hyphenate when a base word begins with a capital letter :: Hyphenate when two like vowels come together :: Hyphenate most words with the prefixes **self-** and **ex-** :: Hyphenate the prefix **re-** whenever necessary to distinguish from words otherwise spelled identically

32. Hyphenate numbers from twenty-one through ninety-nine   92

33. The apostrophe with **s** shows the possessive case   93
   Singular nouns that end in a sound other than **s** or **z** add an apostrophe and **s** to form the possessive case :: Plural nouns ending in a sound other than **s** or **z** add an apostrophe and **s** to form the possessive case :: Singular nouns ending in an **s** or **z** sound may add an apostrophe and **s** to form the possessive case :: Most plural nouns ending in an **s** or **z** sound add the apostrophe alone to show the possessive case :: Possessive forms of pronouns

34. The apostrophe with **s** is used to show the plural of letters and numerals only   96

35. The apostrophe stands for the omission of letters or numerals — 97
36. Abbreviations — 98
37. Arbitrary uses of commas — 99
    Letters :: Names :: Addresses and place names :: Dates :: Numbers
38. Slant, or virgule — 102
39. Arbitrary uses of the colon — 102
    Salutations in business letters :: Subtitles :: Time telling
40. Capitalization — 103
    Proper names :: First words in sentences, quotations, and lines of poetry :: First and main words in titles :: First-person pronoun
41. Italicization — 111
    Italicizing for emphasis :: Titles of books, plays, motion pictures, long poems, works of art, and periodicals :: Foreign words and phrases :: Words referred to as words :: Minor uses of italics

PART III. Punctuating Imaginative Writing — 115

42. Punctuating dialogue — 116
43. Narration by a fictional character — 117
44. Narration from the point of view of a character's thoughts — 118
45. Direct quotation of a character's thoughts — 119
46. Capitalization — 122
47. Quoting other works in a fictional context — 122
48. Compound words — 123
49. Paragraph length — 124
50. Summary of punctuation in fiction — 124
51. Poetry — 125

Alphabetical Reference Guide — 129

Self-Tests

For Sections 1 through 3	8
For Section 4	10
For Sections 5 through 13	25
For Section 14	29
For Sections 15 and 16	33
For Section 17	36
For Section 18	39
For Section 19	43
For Sections 20 through 22	50
For Sections 23 and 24	57
For Section 25	61
Answers	76

How to Use This Book

If you're in a hurry and simply need a brief review of the right way to use a certain punctuation mark — such as the apostrophe or semicolon — turn to the Alphabetical Reference Guide at the end of this book. Here you'll find a short summary of how each mark is used, along with examples and common errors to avoid. You'll also find a cross reference to other parts of *The Way to Punctuate* where the mark is explained in more detail.

But if you're interested in increasing your knowledge and mastery of punctuation — and most people need to do this — then study Part I ("Punctuating Standard Prose Sentences") from beginning to end. The individual sections are specially arranged to lead you from the simplest to the more complicated uses. Each section builds logically on the preceding one. When you have finished, you will have a grasp of how punctuation is actually a part of sentence meaning. You will know how to use punctuation marks to make your meaning clear, and how to tailor punctuation to the structure of a sentence.

Don't try to memorize rules for each punctuation mark separately. Doing this is going at the problem backwards. Instead, learn *why* certain marks are used in certain places, and learn how to choose exactly the right mark for your needs. Sometimes a rule won't help. You may have a choice among several ways to punctuate a given sentence.

The Way to Punctuate recognizes that words and sentences come first, and appropriate punctuation is fitted to them. This book differs from other manuals of punctuation in its logical laying-out of sentence patterns that everyone uses. When you master the patterns you can see how to punctuate them properly. Grammatical terms are unavoidable, but are used sparingly and explained when necessary.

In addition to punctuating sentences, certain marks also have arbitrary uses that must simply be memorized—the apostrophe, for example, to show possession, or capitalization to indicate a proper noun. These arbitrary uses have all been collected together in Part II, where they can be referred to separately. They have little bearing on the problems of punctuating sentences. For example, it doesn't make sense to read about how commas are used in separating parts of long numbers (like 1,342,624) when you are studying how to use commas or semicolons in separating parts of a sentence. Arbitrary uses are therefore arranged so they do not interfere with your development of skill in the art of punctuating standard prose.

Finally, *The Way to Punctuate* shows you how novelists and poets use punctuation in special imaginative ways. The beginning writer ordinarily has no place to turn for an explanation of these uses, and must simply gather his knowledge from reading and by trial and error. Now you can see the reasons behind special imaginative punctuation, and how it is related to standard usage.

The Way to Punctuate has eliminated discussion of some highly conservative and outmoded practices. It is aimed at acceptable and common usage for today. For example, "sentence fragments" are frowned upon by English teachers everywhere. True, there are *kinds* of sentence fragments which must be avoided, and these are clearly explained. But there are legitimately incomplete sentences of a type you will find in wide popular use, and these are also explained so that you can confidently learn the difference. Current acceptable practices, rather than time-honored conventions, have been followed throughout.

Punctuation has long been considered the stronghold of inflexible and prescriptive rules. This tradition is unfortunate. To a great degree, punctuation is variable, flexible, and even imaginative. It is not difficult to understand. You can learn to use it to your own best advantage.

THE WAY TO PUNCTUATE

PART I
Punctuating Standard Prose Sentences

A short and simple sentence requires no punctuation except at the end. If all sentences were simple enough, no commas or other internal punctuation would be necessary. But such simple sentences are too limited to express our thoughts all the time, and we inevitably begin to use more complicated sentence patterns that require commas (and a few other marks) to show which words or word groups must go together and which must be kept separate. Punctuation is an indispensable guide for keeping the meaning clear and for indicating exact shades of meaning that would otherwise be lost.

Fortunately, there are only a few *kinds* of complication behind all the many particular uses of commas and other internal marks. Only four basic principles govern more than 90 per cent of all the punctuation marks you need to use in standard prose writing. These principles are:

1. The separation of items arranged in series or compounded in other ways,

2. The separation of items moved from their normal place in the sentence order,

3. The separation of so-called nonrestrictive modifiers (descriptive elements that are not necessary to the basic sentence),

4. The separation of interruptive elements that are not a part of the basic sentence pattern.

2 • Standard Prose Sentences

You need not memorize these principles, for the best way to learn them is through example and practice. This chapter breaks down these principles into a step-by-step series of practical rules that you can apply to any sentence you write.

Don't begin by trying to memorize all the various punctuation marks and their customary uses. This procedure goes at the problem backwards, although it is the way many people try to master it. For better results, learn which places in a sentence need a punctuation mark—and why. Then you can intelligently choose the right mark that exactly suits your need. You will possess the flexibility and good judgment that make for clear and easy writing.

Of course, complete mastery of punctuation goes further than the four basic principles listed above. But the finer and more complicated points are presented toward the end of this chapter, in order for you to master the basic and most useful patterns first.

1. PLACE A COMMA AFTER EACH ITEM IN A SERIES

Almost any single element in a sentence can be multiplied into a string of three or more to produce a series. For example, take the subject of a verb. The following sentence has only a single subject:

Dimes are no longer made of pure silver.

We can compound, or double, the subject:

Dimes and *quarters* are no longer made of pure silver.

We can also triple the subject:

Dimes and *quarters* and *half-dollars* are no longer made of pure silver.

However, when we reach three items, the word "and" begins to seem overused and repetitious. Instead, we substitute commas:

1. Commas in series • 3

Dimes, quarters, and half-dollars are no longer made of pure silver.

Notice that a comma is used after the word "quarters," even though it does not replace "and" in that position. The reason is simple and sensible. We want to show that *all three* items are separate and have equal rank. If we were to omit the second comma, it would tend to look as though the last two formed a pair rather than part of a series:

quarters and half-dollars

By placing a comma after "quarters," we break up such an unintended pair and show that all three items have equal rank:

Dimes, quarters, and half-dollars

Some writers, on the other hand, argue that the last comma is not necessary, because it duplicates the function of "and," and because most readers would not take the last two items to be a pair anyway. You may omit the comma if you wish, as some writers, editors, and teachers prefer to do, particularly in newspaper and magazine articles:

My great-grandfather acquired in this way the house, the farm and the quarry.

Still, there are better reasons for using the last comma. Most important is our mental habit of seeing the word "and" as a connector that coordinates *two* equal things, setting up a pair rather than a series. It is worthwhile to maintain this distinction. When we read "quarters and half-dollars" or "the farm and the quarry," we may expect to be dealing with a coordinate *pair* rather than with the last two items of a coordinate *series*. If you follow the practice of always omitting the comma before "and," you have no way of distinguishing whether such a pair is intentional or accidental. For example:

They were served coffee, muffins and jam, ham and eggs.

4 • Standard Prose Sentences

There are only three items in the series, but the writer intends two of them to be read as pairs:

muffins and jam
ham and eggs

If he had intended to distribute each separate item individually, he would have written:

They were served coffee, muffins, jam, ham, and eggs.

"Ham and eggs" is a unit, whereas "ham, and eggs" are two separate things.

Notice what happens when the comma is omitted from a series that includes such pairs:

They were served coffee, muffins and jam and ham and eggs.

The two pairs read like a sequence of four separate items, and the point of the series is lost. Furthermore, the use of the comma enables you to drop one of the "and's," thereby reducing repetition. The connective "and" is often dropped from a series for purposes of simplicity and emphasis:

Mrs. Post has produced a world which has its characters, its atmosphere, its drama.

Other linking words—"or" or "nor"—may also be used in a series. The comma is used the same as it is with "and":

These questions are usually expressed in terms of doubt, indecision, or inner struggle.

Barclay had neither friends, followers, nor money.

To summarize: place a comma after each item in a series. Journalistic and informal usage often omits the comma before the connective word (*and, or, nor*). More conservative and careful usage requires it, in order to maintain the distinction between items arranged in a series and items arranged in pairs. A comma is *not* placed between two items intended to be read as a coordinate pair.

2. HOW TO AVOID THREE COMMON ERRORS IN PUNCTUATING A SERIES

First: When a series functions as the multiple subject of a verb, do not use a comma after the very last word in the series:

Dimes, quarters, and half-dollars are no longer made of pure silver. [NO comma after "half-dollars."]

A subject is normally not separated from its verb by a single comma. You would not write

Half-dollars, are no longer made of pure silver. [Omit the comma.]

For the same reason, no comma is used after the last item when the subject happens to be a series rather than a single word.

Second: Do not use a comma or colon before the first word in the series.

WRONG: These questions are usually expressed in terms of, doubt, indecision, or inner struggle. [Omit comma after "of."]

WRONG: These questions are usually expressed in terms of: doubt, indecision, and inner struggle. [Omit colon after "of."]

The comma or colon in these examples is sometimes mistakenly believed to represent a pause in speaking. But pauses cannot always be depended on as a guide in punctuation. Sometimes, it is true, punctuation marks do coincide with pauses or changes in voice level. Our system of punctuation, however, is not based on a complete or regular correspondence with spoken English. Don't assume that a pause necessarily calls for a comma.

The misuse of the comma and colon before a series may also result from mistaking this kind of series for a list of items preceded by an introductory statement. Ordinarily, a series is created by multiplying some single element in the sentence, such as a subject, a verb, an adjective, or adverb. The series is

6 • Standard Prose Sentences

therefore a continuous and integrated part of the sentence, not separated from the rest of the sentence by a comma or colon. See Section 24, page 55, for correct use of the colon preceding a list.

Third: Do not use a comma *after* the connective word in a series, such as "and" or "or."

>WRONG: These questions are usually expressed in terms of doubt, indecision, or, inner struggle. [Omit comma *after* "or."]

Here again the comma may be mistakenly believed to represent a pause in speaking. Even if you would pause for emphasis at that point, do not place a comma there.

3. DO NOT SEPARATE TWO COORDINATE WORDS OR PHRASES WITH A COMMA

You are now familiar with a basic principle: Three or more items in a series are separated by commas. But pairs of two are not.

A pair of subjects:

>Time and tide wait for no man.
>WRONG: Time, and tide, wait for no man. [Omit commas.]

A pair of verbs:

>Birds sang and fluttered in the leafy hedge.
>WRONG: Birds sang, and fluttered, in the leafy hedge. [Omit commas.]

A pair of direct objects:

>Snow whitened the rooftops and lawns.
>WRONG: Snow whitened the rooftops, and lawns. [Omit comma.]

A pair of adjectives:

3. Coordinate words • 7

McGregor's face was white and angry.
WRONG: McGregor's face was white, and angry. [Omit comma.]

A pair of phrases:

Larry knocked the ball over the shed and into the tree.
WRONG.: Larry knocked the ball over the shed, and into the tree. [Omit comma.]

If the two coordinate items are quite lengthy or loaded with modifiers, a comma may be placed between them for clarity. For example, the following sentence has two verbs with a single subject:

The house stands at the end of Edgewater Street with a sweeping view of the beach and bay, and will not be difficult to sell.

The following sentence has two coordinate noun clauses beginning with "that." Their length requires a comma between them for clarity:

Two of Forster's main ideas are that poetry, mystery, passion, ecstasy, music do indeed count, and that personal relationships are a good deal more important than public duty.

Even two short items may be separated by a comma for greater emphasis:

The whale heaved its head from the water, and struck.

Or for negative contrast:

She cried a lot afterward, but recovered.

Nevertheless, use such commas sparingly and only when they add clarity and force to your sentence. The following sentence demonstrates how easy it is to do without commas even when four sets of coordinate pairs are involved:

Grants will be available to American elementary- and

8 • Standard Prose Sentences

secondary-school teachers and to college instructors and assistant professors to teach abroad during the academic year or to attend a seminar abroad during the summer.

Self-Test

Place commas where necessary in the following sentences. *Not all sentences contain a series of three or more items.* Place commas only in those sentences which require them.

1. Norman Mailer is Hemingway's great disciple rival admirer and critic.
2. The frightened snake hissed and struck.
3. The frightened snake coiled hissed and struck.
4. Alice was neither wife sister nor mother.
5. Norman Mailer is Hemingway's great disciple and admirer.
6. Rain high winds and falling temperatures are predicted for the Middle West.
7. Maturity and intelligence are two characteristics of a leader.
8. The village was small lonely and isolated.
9. They wasted their time their effort their money.
10. Conflicts have occurred between students and faculty students and administration and faculty and administration.

(Answers on p. 76.)

4. HOW TO PLACE COMMAS IN A STRING OF MODIFIERS

The same basic principle that applies to any other series applies also to a series of adjectives. If the adjectives all modify the noun separately and with equal rank—that is, if they are all coordinate adjectives—a comma is placed after each one:

4. Commas and modifiers • 9

>The village was small, lonely, and isolated.

When a series of adjectives comes before the noun, the connective word "and" is frequently omitted:

>They lived in a small, lonely, isolated village.

Even when only two coordinate adjectives precede a noun, separate them with a comma if "and" is omitted (the comma replaces "and"):

>They lived in a lonely, isolated village.

But if the two adjectives are linked with "and," the comma is not needed:

>They lived in a lonely and isolated village.

DO NOT put a comma after the last adjective preceding the noun.

>WRONG: They lived in a small, lonely, isolated, village. [Omit the comma after "isolated." The word "village" is not a part of the series of adjectives.]

Use commas, then, in a string of adjectives when each one is given clear and separate emphasis.

Commas may be omitted, however, when the modifiers and noun seem more closely related, and blending is desired rather than separation:

>a tired old man
>a clear blue sky

This construction occurs often when a modifier and noun form a unit of meaning—"old man," "blue sky"—and the first adjective seems to apply to both of them.

Such strings of modifiers can be extended to great lengths without commas:

>Dorothea wore a dark gray wool coat.
>Dorothea wore an old shabby gray wool coat.
>We had a delicious creamy French cheese for dessert.

10 • Standard Prose Sentences

But if the modifiers do not relate closely to each other and are intended to have individual separate emphasis, commas are necessary:

> He gave a spirited, original, provocative performance.

Finally, adjectives may be grouped in pairs, just like the noun combinations "ham and eggs" and "muffins and jam":

> The blossoms may be lavender, blue, red and white, or yellow and white.

Some of the blossoms are a combination of red and white, and some are a combination of yellow and white. Others are all lavender or all blue. The series contains two pairs of adjectives.

Self-Test

Insert commas only where necessary in the following sentences. Not all of the sentences contain a series requiring commas.

1. Antonio's grandmother was very short black-haired and extremely thin.
2. Tiny green insects buzzed at the window.
3. She played with all her little toy animals.
4. Roderick Usher dwelt in an ancient decaying mansion.
5. It was an expensive cigarette lighter.
6. Several brilliant yellow autumn leaves lay on the steps.

(Answers on p. 77.)

5. HOW TO PLACE COMMAS IN A SERIES OF WORD GROUPS

You are already familiar with one of the simplest kinds of word groups: a pair of words connected by "and," such as "ham and eggs" and "red and white" in the sentences above. Other kinds of phrases may also be arranged in a series:

5. Commas and word groups • 11

> At any speed it can move *toward the observer, away from the observer,* or *in a straight path.*

Each phrase or word group is a unit and is followed by a comma just as if it were a single word.

Sometimes both single words and word groups are mixed in the same series:

> At any speed it can move horizontally, vertically, toward the observer, away from the observer, in a straight path, a zigzag, a spiral.

The simpler items are usually placed first, with the more complicated ones at the end. In the example above, the two single words "horizontally" and "vertically" come first; then, the two phrases "toward the observer" and "away from the observer." Finally, the writer places the most complicated group at the end: "in a straight path, a zigzag, a spiral." By arranging this series in a column, we can see more clearly how it is organized:

> horizontally,
> vertically,
> toward the observer,
> away from the observer,
> in a straight path, a zigzag, a spiral.

Notice that the last word group is actually a smaller subordinate series within the larger one. The writer means to say, "in a straight path, in a zigzag, or in a spiral." But in order to avoid repeating the word "in," he condenses the three phrases into a series of objects of the preposition "in," and omits the connective word "or."

A series of word groups may also function as the compound subject of a verb, just as a series of single words may do. To refresh your memory, review the sentence with which we began:

> Dimes, quarters, and half-dollars are no longer made of pure silver.

12 • Standard Prose Sentences

You will recall that a comma is *not* placed after the last word of the series, between subject and verb. A comma there would create a meaningless and unnecessary break. Now notice the difference when the series consists of word groups:

> George Herbert in his quiet Wiltshire parish, John Donne in the deanery of St. Paul's, or Jeremy Taylor in the calm retirement of the Golden Grove, enjoyed advantages denied the pioneer Bostonian.

Strictly speaking, a comma should not follow "Golden Grove," which marks the end of the third word group. But the series is quite long, and the reader could easily fail to notice that it had ended, except for the comma. Without it, the last word group alone would seem to take over as subject of the verb, leaving the first two dangling. In order to show that all three word groups are coordinate and equal, a comma is placed after each of them.

We can illustrate this principle again by expanding one of our previous simple examples into a more complicated series of word groups.

> SIMPLE: Rain, high winds, and falling temperatures are predicted for the Middle West.
>
> MORE COMPLICATED: Rain mixed with sleet or hail, high winds up to fifty-five miles per hour, and falling temperatures in the range of thirty-five to forty-five degrees, are predicted for the Middle West.

If a comma creates an interruption between subject and verb, then it should be avoided as a hazard to clarity. On the other hand, if it is necessary to define the end of a long and complicated subject, it should be used.

6. USE SEMICOLONS TO SEPARATE ITEMS IN MORE COMPLICATED SERIES

Sometimes commas are not adequate to mark the breaks between word groups in a series. If word groups happen to contain commas within themselves, such commas tend to obscure

6. Semicolons and series • 13

the larger break between word groups as a whole. The reader needs to be shown clearly the distinction between the minor divisions and the larger ones. Commas can't be used for both. Semicolons are therefore used to mark the end of word groups, while commas are used for the lesser divisions within those groups:

> Sightings of flying saucers were reported at Windom, Minnesota; Cherokee, Iowa; Omaha, Nebraska; Springfield, Missouri; Smackover, Arkansas; and Baton Rouge, Louisiana.

If commas only were used, the series would look like this:

> Windom, Minnesota, Cherokee, Iowa, Omaha, Nebraska, Springfield, Missouri, Smackover, Arkansas, and Baton Rouge, Louisiana.

Before you reach the end, the sentence begins to read like a series of single words, as if the states and cities had equal rank. No distinction is made between the word groups and the single words within the groups, because commas are used for both degrees of separation.

The same problem arises when one of the word groups in a series contains a smaller series of items within itself. Again, this construction requires two *kinds* of separation: a smaller separation within the word group and a larger one between the word groups themselves. Again, the semicolon comes to the rescue:

> The flying saucer may be white, black, gray, red, blue, green, pink, yellow, silver; may be luminous or dull; may be a solid color; may be circled by a central band of different color; may display flashing lights of various colors.

The first word group contains eight commas. But the writer must make it clear that these eight commas mark the breaks within that one word group alone and are not a part of a larger sequence of breaks in the sentence as a whole. Semicolons mark the larger divisions.

14 • Standard Prose Sentences

An extremely long series of word groups is always rendered more clear if semicolons are used for separation, even when there are only a few commas within the individual word groups. Semicolons form emphatic breaks and give the reader's eye a resting point, enabling him to keep each word group distinctly separate in his mind:

> At different times and places it may be a circular disk like a saucer, often with a small protrusion in the center like a knob on a teakettle lid; elliptical or bean-shaped like a flattened sphere; a circular base supporting a dome-like superstructure; a sphere surrounded by a central platform, like Saturn in its rings; long and thin like a cigar; a tapered sphere like a teardrop; spindle-shaped, with or without knobs on the ends; or a double- or triple-decked form like a stack of plates.

Self-Test

In the following sentence, place semicolons between the main divisions of the series and commas between the minor ones:

Building a better community improved education better understanding of the free enterprise system an effective attack on heart ailments emphysema alcoholism or other crippling diseases participation in the political party of choice and renewed emphasis on regular religious observances are all examples of such further goals.

(Answers on p. 77.)

7. USE A COMMA BETWEEN SENTENCES CONNECTED BY <u>AND</u>, <u>BUT</u>, <u>OR</u>, <u>NOR</u>, OR <u>YET</u>

These connective words are called "coordinating conjunctions," because they coordinate or balance equally two or

7. Commas and conjunctions • 15

more elements. You have already seen how they coordinate two items to form pairs:

lonely and isolated
tired but happy
right or wrong
neither wife nor mother
wealthy yet powerless

They also coordinate the items in a series:

red, white, and blue
red, white, or blue
neither red, white, nor blue
thin, light, but strong
thin, light, yet strong

In exactly the same way, these conjunctions may be used to coordinate two complete sentences:

The large corporation is a complex organization, and individuals align themselves with its goals for many reasons.

Two sentences should be so joined only when they share a continuous and integrated thought. The conjunction is not used just to string sentences together like beads, but to show a relationship of connection or contrast:

I did not know what I could do, but I wanted to see what was happening.
The nations must learn to live together, or they will face total destruction.
Grandfather Baker would not consider selling the house, nor would he even consent to renting it.
It must be an essay, yet it is longer than that.

Notice two things:
The comma always goes just before the conjunction — never after it.
A comma is used even when there are only two sentences. It does not require a series of three or more.

16 • Standard Prose Sentences

The most common error is to place the comma after the conjunction rather than before it.

>   WRONG: I did not know what I could do but, I wanted to see what was happening. [Shift the comma to the position before "but."]
>   WRONG: I did not know what I could do, but, I wanted to see what was happening. [Retain the comma before "but," but eliminate the one after it.]

The latter error probably occurs through a mistaken belief that the comma after the conjunction represents a pause in speaking. Even though you might pause for emphasis after the word "but," do not place a comma there when writing. The comma goes before the conjunction.

Although it is standard practice to use a comma whenever two sentences are joined by a conjunction, the comma can occasionally be omitted if the sentences are simple, short, and closely integrated in meaning:

>   Hailstones broke the kitchen windows and rain flooded the basement.

You may also follow standard practice and use a comma to separate such sentences. The effect of the comma is to add emphasis:

>   Hailstones broke the kitchen windows, and rain flooded the basement.

If the subjects of the verbs in the two sentences are similar or identical, the two sentences are obviously more closely related than usual and the comma can be omitted:

>   The nations must learn to live together or they will face total destruction.

However, if you feel any uncertainty in deciding whether a comma should be used, then use it. You won't be wrong.

8. DO NOT CONNECT SENTENCES WITH A COMMA ALONE

A comma should not be used as a substitute for a conjunction when two sentences are joined.

> WRONG: The large corporation is a complex organization, individuals align themselves with its goals for many reasons. [Insert "and" after the comma.]

This error is called a "comma splice."

You may feel that a comma splice isn't *always* wrong. Perhaps you have even seen it in print. One legitimate use of the comma splice is the arrangement of three or more simple sentences in a series, like Caesar's famous "I came, I saw, I conquered":

> She haggles, she niggles, she wears out our patience with her repetitions and her prolixities.

Notice, however, that in both these examples the subject of each of the three sentences is the same and is repeated only for stylistic effect. They could have been written as an ordinary series of verbs with a single subject:

> I came, saw, and conquered.
> She haggles, niggles, and wears out our patience with her repetitions and prolixities.

If the subject is not the same, such series should be used sparingly and only when the sentence structures are parallel and closely related in meaning:

> Lightning flashed, thunder roared, and rain beat at the windows.

Such a series should not be created by thoughtlessly putting together any sequence of sentences.

WRONG: The house was built by the Johnsons, they owned the large farm, they also had a profitable grist mill.

This sequence of sentences should not be connected with commas, for the sentences do not constitute a meaningful series. Instead, they should be grouped and separated according to their logical relationship.

CORRECT: The house was built by the Johnsons, who owned the large farm. They also had a profitable grist mill.

Imaginative literature also allows use of the comma splice to attain special stylistic effects. For example, dialogue in fiction may deliberately use the comma splice in order to show how two statements are run together with only a slight pause in speaking:

"I don't know why he picked on me, I just asked a simple question."

Descriptive writing, too, may employ the comma splice in order to attain an emotional effect:

Time did not exist, space did not exist—only the blackness of infinity.

In both these examples, the comma splice allows the writer to juxtapose two sentences without actually stating the logical connection between them. The connection, however, is clearly understood:

"I don't know why he picked on me, [because] I just asked a simple question."

Time did not exist, [and] space did not exist—only the blackness of infinity.

Such condensation can sometimes be more expressive than conventional usage would be, but it should be tried only by a writer who knows exactly how the comma is normally used and why he is departing from normal usage. For further advice on how to break the rules intelligently, see Part III: Punctuat-

ing Imaginative Writing. In writing standard prose, do not try to use the comma splice deliberately. It is out of place.

9. A SEMICOLON MAY BE USED BETWEEN SENTENCES IN PLACE OF A COMMA

Sometimes the writer wishes to indicate a stronger break between sentences connected by a coordinating conjunction than a comma is able to indicate. In such cases, a semicolon is used in exactly the same position as the comma:

> The huge root of an elm has split the thick slabs of the pavement so that you have to walk over a hump; and one of the big square stone fence-posts is toppling.

A comma would be equally correct, but would not create such a decided break. The writer wished to separate and emphasize each of the points he was making, but at the same time wished to show their relationship.

A semicolon rather than a comma is often used in a series of complete sentences:

> It has dissolved some of its most important functions; it has greatly narrowed its area of action; and it has bent its residual operations very largely to its own needs.

The connective word "and" may be omitted from such series, as you have already seen:

> He was not taken into Lord Leicester's service; he was not made Public Orator; he was not given the Mastership of Trinity Hall.

Either of these sentences could have been written more simply, and commas could have been used instead of semicolons. But the writers wished to place heavy emphasis on each separate statement in the series.

10. A SEMICOLON MAY ALSO SUBSTITUTE FOR A CONJUNCTION

A semicolon may do what a comma may not do: it may substitute for an omitted conjunction. In the example below, the omitted conjunction "but" is understood, and the semicolon takes its place.

None denies that the corporations could make higher returns by raising prices; the policy rests firmly on the fact that they do not maximize returns.

In the following case, "and" is omitted and replaced by the semicolon.

We go in swimming; it is miles away from anywhere.

To repeat: A comma *cannot* be used in this fashion to stand alone between two sentences. The comma must be used along with a coordinating conjunction, unless the sentences form a proper series, or some imaginative use is involved. But the semicolon *can* take the place of a conjunction.

11. PLACE A COMMA AFTER AN INTRODUCTORY OR TRANSITIONAL EXPRESSION

A careful writer frequently begins his sentences with transitional expressions like "nevertheless," "however," "moreover," "for example." Such expressions refer to the thought in the previous sentence while forming a logical transition to the following one:

Nonetheless, a movement ought to be judged by its best rather than its worst representatives.
However, the question must be allowed to rest at this point.
Still, it is the only property I have owned.

11. Transitional expressions • 21

Such expressions may be phrases as well as single words:

> After all, what laws can be laid down about books?
> To be sure, some scientists have argued that there may be no incompatibility.
> In summary, the industrial system has built into itself very comprehensively the need to regulate aggregate demand.

The comma in such cases always indicates a voice pause, which in speaking separates the transitional phrase from the rest of the sentence. This is important to remember, since some adverbs are not always transitional and therefore do not always require commas. In the following example, "however" and "still" are NOT used to show transition. They are not separated by a voice pause and do not require commas:

> However you interpret his remarks, they are still derogatory.

12. PLACE A PAIR OF COMMAS AROUND A TRANSITIONAL EXPRESSION WHEN IT IS MOVED FURTHER ON INTO THE SENTENCE

Expressions inserted within the normal flow of the sentence are usually interruptive. They are therefore enclosed by commas both before and after. When a transitional expression is moved from the beginning of the sentence to a position further along, commas ordinarily enclose it.

> EXAMPLE: Every legend, moreover, contains its residuum of truth.
> ALTERNATIVE: Moreover, every legend contains its residuum of truth.
> EXAMPLE: Consider, for example, Houdini's report to Arthur Conan Doyle.
> ALTERNATIVE: For example, consider Houdini's report to Arthur Conan Doyle.

Such commas must come in pairs. A frequent error is to omit one of the two necessary commas, leaving the interruptive expression open at one end.

> WRONG: Consider for example, Houdini's report to Arthur Conan Doyle. [Place a comma after "consider."]

Occasionally the transitional expression may seem so closely tied in with the rest of the sentence that it does not need to be set off with commas.

> EXAMPLE: The results nevertheless are interesting.
> ALTERNATIVE: The results, nevertheless, are interesting.
> EXAMPLE: Consider for example Houdini's report to Arthur Conan Doyle.
> ALTERNATIVE: Consider, for example, Houdini's report to Arthur Conan Doyle.

In such borderline cases, both ways are correct, although modern usage prefers to eliminate such commas unless they are absolutely necessary for clarity.

In deciding whether to use commas or not, you must judge how seriously the expression interrupts the sentence. If you choose to omit commas, then omit both of them — not just one. If you choose to use them, then use both of them — not just one.

13. DO NOT MISTAKE A TRANSITIONAL WORD FOR A CONJUNCTION

Transitional adverbs like "however," "nevertheless," and "therefore" are used to show the logical relationship between two sentences. "However" tells the reader that the sentence is going to state an exception to what has gone before. "Nevertheless" indicates that the sentence is going to assert the truth of something in spite of what has gone before. "Therefore" indicates that the sentence will state the result of some cause that has gone before. Such adverbs usually come at the beginning of the sentence, or very near it, as you have already seen:

13. Transitional words vs. conjunctions • 23

> Three automobiles were involved in the accident. However, no one was seriously injured.
>
> Protesters have besieged the college for two days. Nevertheless, the president intends to keep classes in session.
>
> Expressions inserted within the normal flow of the sentence are interruptive. Therefore, they are enclosed by commas both before and after.

Very often the writer wishes to combine both sentences into one. At this point you will recall that two sentences can be combined in only two ways: by a conjunction or by a semicolon. Transitional adverbs are not conjunctions. Their function is logical, not grammatical. Therefore, they cannot serve as the grammatical connector of the sentences. The solution is to use a semicolon:

> Three automobiles were involved in the accident; however, no one was seriously injured.
>
> Protesters have besieged the college for two days; nevertheless, the president intends to keep classrooms open.
>
> Expressions inserted within the normal flow of the sentence are interruptive; therefore, they are enclosed by commas both before and after.

See how such a sentence would look if a conjunction were used instead of a semicolon:

> Protesters have besieged the college for two days, but, nevertheless, the president intends to keep classrooms open.

Nothing is gained in meaning by adding the conjunction "but," since the adverb "nevertheless" already implies contrast between the two statements. Such duplication of meaning is pointless and wordy. It is best to use either a conjunction or a transitional adverb, but not both at once. If you choose the conjunction, you may use a comma:

> Protesters have besieged the college for two days, but the president intends to keep classrooms open.

24 • Standard Prose Sentences

If you choose the adverb, you *must* use a semicolon, since there is no other grammatical connection between the sentences:

> Protesters have besieged the college for two days; nevertheless, the president intends to keep classrooms open.

A comma alone cannot be used for the connection. To do so would create a comma splice.

> WRONG: Three automobiles were involved in the accident, however, no one was seriously injured. [Change the comma after "accident" to a semicolon.]

The same principle applies, of course, to any other transitional word or phrase. The following lists show some of the most common ones you are likely to use:

again	then
also	therefore
besides	thus
consequently	for example
furthermore	for that reason
however	in fact
indeed	on the other hand
instead	that is
likewise	in any case
meanwhile	in summary
moreover	after all
nevertheless	in short
otherwise	of course
still	

REMINDER: Such expressions are not always transitional. Be guided by voice pause, which indicates that the word or phrase is interruptive. In the following examples, expressions drawn from the above lists are *not* used to show transitions, but are simply adverbs modifying other words in the sentences:

> I am indeed pleased to be here.

I am otherwise engaged for the afternoon.
We will again offer three overseas programs.

Self-Test
Write two related sentences, beginning the second one with "meanwhile." Then join them with a semicolon. Repeat this exercise three times, using three other transitional expressions from the above lists.

Insert commas or semicolons where necessary in the following sentences, all of which consist of two or more independent sentences joined together.

1. They played tennis they went for afternoon walks they read novels by the dozen but time passed with agonizing slowness.
2. Berlin fell and the Third Reich fell with it.
3. Summers in Death Valley are unbelievably hot but the animal life is remarkably adapted for survival.
4. The climbing party finally reached a broad ledge on the southwest side of the peak here they could rest and regain strength.
5. The stock market fluctuated according to news of the war that is it rose with each victory and dropped with each setback.

The following sentences are incorrectly punctuated. Remove commas or semicolons from places where they are wrong and add them where they are necessary.

6. Rescue parties attempted to enter the mine three times during the night but, poisonous gases or fire drove them back.
7. Red China has indicated its willingness to resume talks, however, the State Department doubts its sincerity.
8. In any case; you must file your tax return by April 15.

(Answers on pp. 77–78.)

14. HOW TO USE COMMAS WITH OTHER MOVABLE PHRASES

You are now familiar with introductory and transitional phrases, such as "on the other hand" and "for example." They can occur at the beginning of the sentence:

> For example, hospital charges have increased 122%.

They can occur in midsentence:

> Hospital charges, for example, have increased 122%.

They can even occur at the end:

> Hospital charges have increased 122%, for example.

(This last example is not as good, since it forces the reader to wait too long for the logical connection. But it is not incorrect.)

Such phrases are interrupters and are normally set off with commas—with one comma if the phrase occurs at the beginning or the end, and with two commas if it occurs in midsentence.

Not all phrases are interrupters. They may be an integral part of the sentence:

> The winner chose an automatic washer instead of money as her prize.

The phrase "instead of money" is in its normal position in the sentence. No comma is needed to set it off. We expect such phrases to follow the words they modify as closely as possible.

But such phrases may be moved to other positions in the sentence, either for greater emphasis, for variety in sentence pattern, or for a better logical relationship between sentences. Once out of their normally expected position, they must usually be set apart with commas:

> Instead of money, the winner chose an automatic washer.
> [The phrase is at the beginning of the sentence. One comma is needed after it.]

14. Commas and movable phrases • 27

The winner chose, instead of money, an automatic washer as her prize. [The phrase is in midsentence. Two commas are needed, one before and one after.]

The separation of such phrases by commas will insure that the sentence remains clear despite the changed order of the phrases. Often the shift of a phrase to another position creates no problem of clarity or awkwardness, and commas can be omitted:

> NORMAL POSITION: He always wore a necktie at work.
> SHIFTED POSITION: At work he always wore a necktie.
> NORMAL POSITION: The children were awake before seven o'clock.
> SHIFTED POSITION: Before seven o'clock the children were awake.

But if you omit the comma, be sure the movable phrase does not accidentally create confusion by blending with the words that follow.

> NORMAL POSITION: Leaves turn brown in autumn.
> SHIFTED POSITION: In autumn leaves turn brown.

The reader mistakenly reads "In autumn leaves," and then is forced to reread the sentence to discover that a break is intended after "autumn" rather than after "leaves."

> IMPROVED: In autumn, leaves turn brown.

This comma is especially important when the phrase contains a verbal element. The verbal too readily connects to a following word.

> NORMAL POSITION: The animals usually sleep after eating.
> SHIFTED POSITION: After eating the animals usually sleep.

A comma is necessary to avoid the misreading "after eating the animals."

> IMPROVED: After eating, the animals usually sleep.

If a long phrase is shifted to the beginning of a sentence, it is usually advisable to set it off with a comma. A reader's eye usually glances ahead, and the comma provides instant clarity by defining the end of a long phrase.

> NORMAL POSITION: Interest rates continue to rise in spite of repeated warnings by the president's economic advisors.
>
> SHIFTED POSITION: In spite of repeated warnings by the president's economic advisors, interest rates continue to rise.

Such extremely long phrases are not generally placed in mid-sentence, for the simple reason that they force the other elements in the sentence too far apart. But if they are so placed, they require a pair of commas:

> Interest rates, in spite of repeated warnings by the president's economic advisors, continue to rise.

We have been dealing with what are called "prepositional phrases." Such phrases consist of a preposition as a headword followed by its so-called object. Prepositions are words like *in, on, at, to, with, from, by, for*:

> in time
> after hours
> on leaving
> from her mother
> for several reasons
> at work

Prepositional phrases, as you have seen, normally follow the word they modify. When in their normal position, they are not separated by commas. Be sure, then, that you do not use commas unless they are clearly called for. Needless commas clutter a sentence, obscure meaning, and slow the reader.

> RIGHT: She inherited her blue eyes from her mother.

14. Commas and movable phrases • 29

WRONG: She inherited her blue eyes, from her mother. [Omit comma.]
RIGHT: The building on the corner is vacant.
WRONG: The building, on the corner, is vacant. [Omit commas.]
RIGHT: Insulators with cracks in the porcelain should be discarded.
WRONG: Insulators, with cracks in the porcelain, should be discarded. [Omit commas.]

Prepositional phrases require commas in only three situations:
1. When they occur in a series
2. When they are transitional and interruptive
3. When they are moved from their normal position

SERIES: It was a time of hope, of expectation, of anxiety.
TRANSITIONAL: In the meantime, the president plans to continue negotiations.
MOVED FROM NORMAL POSITION: After earning nearly $800,000, he retired. (He retired after earning nearly $800,000.)

Movable phrases out of normal order will be found most often at the beginning of the sentence, sometimes in mid-sentence, and only rarely at the end.

Self-Test

The following sentences contain phrases used in various ways. Place commas only where necessary. Not every sentence requires them.

1. In short the cost of living is higher than ever.
2. By morning the rain had stopped.
3. The cost of living in a large city is higher than ever.
4. The cost of living in other words is higher than ever.
5. After several fruitless attempts the rescue party reached the thirteen men trapped at the 1200-foot level of the mine.

6. The rescue party reached the trapped miners after several fruitless attempts.
7. Police broke through a door at the head of the stairs in the rear of the house.
8. The ship moved cautiously through the fog toward the harbor mouth.
9. This insect can be found in rotting logs under dead leaves and beneath stones.

(Answers on p. 78.)

15. HOW TO USE COMMAS WITH MOVABLE CLAUSES

A "clause" is simply a word group which has both subject and verb, distinguishing it from a phrase. When it stands alone as a separate sentence, it is called an independent clause:

She threw her pills into the wastebasket.

Two independent clauses may be joined with a coordinating conjunction. A comma is then placed between them:

The doctor left the room, and she threw her pills into the wastebasket.

One of the clauses, however, may be joined to the other by a *subordinating* conjunction. This kind of conjunction does not line up the two clauses as equally balanced sentences, but makes one dependent on the other (or subordinate to it):

She threw her pills into the watebasket when the doctor left the room.

The clause "when the doctor left the room" can no longer stand as an independent sentence. The conjunction "when" forces it to be attached to an independent clause. Alone, it is grammatically incomplete—a one-legged sentence that needs to lean on another for support.

15. Commas and movable clauses • 31

Subordinate clauses, like phrases, normally follow the word or word group which they modify. Also like a phrase, this kind of subordinate clause can be moved to other positions in the sentence. And when it is moved, it is usually advisable to set it off with a comma.

NORMAL POSITION: She threw her pills into the wastebasket when the doctor left the room. [No comma is needed.]

SHIFTED POSITION: When the doctor left the room, she threw her pills into the wastebasket. [The comma is required.]

Other commonly used subordinating conjunctions include *if, although, after, because, while, since, unless*:

You may leave if you have finished.
If you have finished, you may leave.
He left although he had not finished.
Although he had not finished, he left.
He left after he had finished.
After he had finished, he left.
He left because he had finished.
Because he had finished, he left.
He left while the others were finishing.
While the others were finishing, he left.
You may leave since the others have finished.
Since the others have finished, you may leave.
You may leave unless you haven't finished.
Unless you haven't finished, you may leave.

Grammatically, such movable clauses are called "adverbial" because they function as single-word adverbs do. But the important thing to remember is that they may be moved to various positions in the sentence. You can tell them from other kinds of clauses by the fact that they can be shifted. When in their normal position following the verb, no comma is required. But when moved to the beginning of the sentence, a comma is placed after them.

If a movable clause is placed in midsentence, it is set off with a pair of commas—one before and one after.

NORMAL POSITION: The president pounded his desk whenever he was angry. [No comma needed.]
BEGINNING OF SENTENCE: Whenever he was angry, the president pounded his desk. [One comma is needed.]
MIDSENTENCE: The president, whenever he was angry, pounded his desk. [A pair of commas is needed.]

Just as with movable phrases, the comma may safely be omitted if the sentence remains clear and no awkwardness results from the omission:

If you are finished you may leave.

But even in such sentences the comma adds emphasis:

If you are finished, you may leave.

And although the comma is normally omitted when the clause comes at the end of the sentence, a comma may nevertheless be desirable if the clause is only loosely related:

They found themselves gradually forgetting the horrifying details of the accident, because time does make a difference.

The comma may also be used to emphasize negative contrast:

He left, although he had not finished.

16. HOW TO USE COMMAS WITH OTHER SENTENCE ELEMENTS OUT OF NORMAL ORDER

Simple adjectives normally precede the noun they modify:

McGregor's pale, angry face appeared in the window.

For stylistic variation, such adjectives may be shifted to a position immediately following their noun:

McGregor's face, pale and angry, appeared in the window.

16. Commas and sentence order

A pair of commas is necessary to set them apart from the sentence.

The adjectives may even be shifted to the end of the sentence:

> McGregor's face appeared in the window, pale and angry.

Again, a comma must separate them from the rest of the sentence.

Reversing the usual sequence of a predicate adjective and a subject ordinarily does not require a comma:

> Great was his disappointment. [His disappointment was great.]

But if two predicate adjectives are separated and distributed in the following manner, use a comma as indicated:

> Vast was his plan, and audacious. [His plan was vast and audacious.]

Unusual reversals of word order, however, quickly become stilted and affected, and punctuation alone cannot make them acceptable even though it may clarify their meaning. Modern writers prefer naturalness.

Self-Test

The following sentences contain movable clauses, some in normal order and some shifted from normal order. Place commas wherever they are needed.

1. Although I disagree with your beliefs I defend your right to express them.
2. Lydia Merivale wore white gloves whenever she left her house.
3. Whenever she left her house Lydia Merivale wore white gloves.
4. Lydia Merivale whenever she left her house wore white gloves.
5. The enemy inflicted 5,748 casualties in one month if we are to believe them.

34 • Standard Prose Sentences

The following sentences contain other elements shifted from their normal position. Place commas wherever they are needed.

6. A profusion of wild flowers purple yellow and white covered the meadow.
7. The eyes in the portrait seemed to follow her cold and accusing.

(Answers on p. 79.)

17. HOW TO USE COMMAS WITH ADJECTIVE CLAUSES

Adjective clauses are not movable; they always follow as closely as possible the nouns they modify. There are two types.

Type 1 must be set off with commas:

Harold Greenacre, who joined the company in 1961, is now regional sales manager.

Type 2 must *not* be set off with commas:

A man who joined the company in 1961 is now regional sales manager.

Type 1 is called *nonrestrictive*, because it does not restrict or limit the noun it modifies to the description contained in the clause. A nonrestrictive clause is merely an additional, nonessential statement. It can be omitted with no loss of basic meaning:

Harold Greenacre is now regional sales manager.

Type 2 is called *restrictive*, because it does restrict the noun to the description contained in the clause. Without this restrictive clause, the preceding noun seems incomplete. It cannot be omitted without losing the intended meaning:

A man is now regional sales manager.

17. Commas with adjective clauses • 35

The clause "who joined the company in 1961" is necessary in order to specify a particular man.

This distinction is perfectly simple and would cause little difficulty if it were not for the terms "restrictive" and "nonrestrictive," which many people find difficult to comprehend accurately. We could just as well term them "essential" and "nonessential." Fortunately, there are several ways to master this problem other than by memorizing terminology.

First, mastering this distinction is one of the few instances in which spoken English is an accurate guide to punctuation. We invariably pause slightly and drop our voice level when speaking or reading aloud a nonrestrictive clause. These pauses and changes in voice level coincide with the commas. Try it with the following sentence:

> The Air Force, which had been hampered by winter storms, resumed its rescue mission in early March. [There is a pause at each comma.]

On the other hand, a restrictive clause is spoken with no pause or drop in voice level:

> The explanation that he gave was not accepted. [There are no pauses before or after the clause "that he gave."]

Second, the restrictive clause sometimes omits the relative pronoun *who, whom, which,* or *that*:

> The explanation he gave was not accepted.

If the relative pronoun can be omitted, the clause is restrictive and therefore requires no commas. (The relative pronoun cannot *always* be omitted from a restrictive clause, but *if* it can be omitted, the clause is certain to be restrictive.)

Third, the relative pronoun "that" is used only with restrictive clauses, never with nonrestrictive ones. If the adjective clause begins with "that," or if you can substitute "that" for *who, whom,* or *which,* then it is restrictive and requires no commas.

Several persons who had witnessed the accident gave conflicting reports.

Several persons that had witnessed the accident gave conflicting reports.

It is possible for the same clause to be treated as either restrictive or nonrestrictive, depending on your intended meaning.

RESTRICTIVE: The Unitarian Church which was built in 1828 will be restored by the Historical Society. [This specifies one particular Unitarian church among others.]

NONRESTRICTIVE: The Unitarian church, which was built in 1828, will be restored by the Historical Society. [There is only one Unitarian Church. The clause only adds some information about it.]

A word of caution: Never place a single comma *after* a restrictive clause.

WRONG: The explanation that he gave, was not accepted.

RIGHT: The explanation that he gave was not accepted.

When an adjective clause comes in midsentence, it requires either a pair of commas or none at all—never a single comma alone.

A few other words, such as *where, when,* or *why,* may also function as the headword of an adjective clause:

The house where we lived in 1953 has been torn down.
He referred to the time when Jackie nearly drowned.
Congress demanded reasons why the war should be continued.

Self-Test

The following sentences contain either restrictive or nonrestrictive clauses. Place commas where they are needed. Apply the three tests if you are in doubt: (1) read the sentence aloud, and use commas to correspond with pauses and change in voice level, (2) try omitting the relative pronoun, (3) try substituting "that" for *who, whom,* or *which.*

1. Poe who is viewed by many as a Southern writer was actually a native of Boston.
2. A Norwegian fishing boat was grounded on the sandbar which lies just outside the entrance to the harbor.
3. The package that we sent on November 10 did not arrive until December 3.
4. The secret was divulged to two newspaper reporters who promptly spread it across the evening headlines.
5. The meadows where cows grazed only ten years ago are now covered with suburban homes.
6. Harry told a joke which she considered offensive.
7. Several villages and one large city lie close to the river which floods on the average of once every twenty-five years.

The following sentences all contain errors. Remove commas used incorrectly and insert commas where they are needed.

8. The money that they counted on for the research project, was voted down by the legislature.
9. The time, when we should have acted, is already past.
10. Several mothers whose sons were in the combat zone, wrote letters to Senator Blackwell who promised to investigate the problem.

(Answers on pp. 79–80.)

18. HOW TO USE COMMAS WITH APPOSITIVES

An appositive is a noun placed immediately after another noun in order to enlarge on its meaning or further identify it:

Adrian Jamieson, a lieutenant, was awarded the Purple Heart.

The appositive in this sentence is "a lieutenant." It re-names the noun that it follows.

Appositives, like adjective clauses, may be either restrictive or nonrestrictive; and the same method is used to tell where to place commas. Listen for the pause and the drop in voice level to tell you that the appositive is nonrestrictive, requiring commas. Most appositives, you will find, are nonrestrictive, like the example above.

The somewhat rarer restrictive appositive has no pause or drop in voice level when spoken aloud:

> His son Bob is a photographer.

This appositive distinguishes Bob from the other sons.

> The class read Katherine Mansfield's story "Bliss."

This appositive distinguishes "Bliss" from other stories by the same author.

Most frequently, appositives are word groups rather than single words—that is, a noun together with its cluster of modifying words:

> Philip Stanhope, Lord Chesterfield's natural son by a Dutch governess, was a little boy of seven.

Noun phrases and clauses, being substitutes for single nouns, may also function as appositives.

> NOUN CLAUSE: His excuse, that his alarm clock hadn't gone off, was not convincing.
>
> INFINITIVE PHRASE: The administration's solution, to suspend the accused students without a hearing, only aroused a more massive protest.

Sometimes the appositive is shifted from its normal position following a noun to a separated position at the end of the sentence:

> Consider what it implies, this art of pleasing.

And sometimes it is placed before the noun, especially in journalistic use:

> A heavy drinker, Gunderson was found dead of alcohol poisoning.

Self-Test

The following sentences contain appositives in various positions. Place commas wherever needed to set off nonrestrictive appositives. Remember that restrictive appositives do not require commas.

1. Her mother the former Madeline Garfield had inherited a fortune in oil and steel.
2. Nineteen sixty-eight a year of unprecedented violence will be recognized as a turning point in American history.
3. A skilled linguist Miller translated his own works into French.
4. My friend Stanley has a summer job in British Columbia.
5. Many persons will be called on for aid particularly those who have had specialized training.
6. The governor's first suggestion to increase revenues by raising student fees was reluctantly withdrawn.

(Answers on p. 80.)

19. HOW TO USE COMMAS WITH VERBAL PHRASES

A "verbal" is a verb form which does not take a subject. There are four kinds:

INFINITIVE: to eat
GERUND: eating
PRESENT PARTICIPLE: eating
PAST PARTICIPLE: eaten

40 • Standard Prose Sentences

Each of these verbals may function as the headword of a phrase.

> INFINITIVE: to eat three meals a day
> GERUND: eating three meals a day
> PRESENT PARTICIPLE: eating three meals a day
> PAST PARTICIPLE: eaten by the animals

Each kind of phrase has its customary use and position in the sentence and therefore its accompanying requirements for punctuation. For the most part, these fall into patterns you are already familiar with.

The infinitive phrase may be used adverbially, like the prepositional phrases you have just studied. Normally, it will then come at the end of the sentence, and no comma is required:

> You don't need an unusual appetite to eat three meals a day.

The adverb phrase may also be shifted to the beginning of the sentence. In this position, it does require a comma:

> To eat three meals a day, you don't need an unusual appetite.

This kind of infinitive phrase requiring the use of a comma is movable; and it has the meaning "in order to."

If the phrase is short, and if no confusion results, the comma may occasionally be omitted:

> To be heard in this room you must shout.

But the comma always adds emphasis and clarity:

> To be heard in this room, you must shout.

One word of caution: Be sure the infinitive phrase at the beginning of the sentence *is* a movable adverb phrase and not a noun phrase serving as subject of the verb.

19. Commas and verbal phrases • 41

RIGHT: To delay the project would be fatal.
WRONG: To delay the project, would be fatal. [Omit comma.]

The phrase "to delay the project" is the subject of the verb "would be." A comma should not separate subject and verb.

But some writers do place a comma after an infinitive phrase as subject if it is unusually long and complicated:

To drive across a 13,000-foot Colorado mountain pass in a blinding snowstorm at zero visibility, is an unforgettable experience.

Strictly speaking, the comma in this sentence is wrong. But it does help the reader identify the place where the lengthy phrasal subject ends and the predicate begins.

A gerund is simply the *-ing* form of the verb used as a noun. It, too, can serve as the headword of a phrase, and is punctuated exactly the same as any other noun group.

No comma follows the noun phrase used as subject:

Delaying the project would be fatal.

The present participle also ends in *-ing* and, by itself, looks exactly the same as a gerund. However, it is used as an adjective, not as a noun. It therefore has different requirements for punctuation.

Participial phrases — which are adjective phrases — may be either restrictive or nonrestrictive, exactly like adjective clauses. When restrictive, they must not be set off with commas:

The boy eating an ice-cream sandwich is Wesley Johnson's son.

The phrase "eating an ice-cream sandwich" distinguishes one boy from the others. It is restrictive.

But when the phrase is nonrestrictive, it requires commas:

Bobby Johnson, eating an ice-cream sandwich, watched the sailboats on the bay.

42 • Standard Prose Sentences

Read the above sentence aloud, and notice that your voice pauses and drops for the nonrestrictive phrase. Listening for pauses is a safe guide for placing commas.

Nonrestrictive phrases are generally movable, and of course continue to require commas when shifted to another position.

NORMAL POSITION: The plane, coming in too low over the hillside, sliced into a clump of trees and crashed.

SHIFTED TO BEGINNING OF SENTENCE: Coming in too low over the hillside, the plane sliced into a clump of trees and crashed.

NORMAL POSITION: The doe and her fawn, browsing on the fresh sprouts, worked their way along the fence.

SHIFTED TO END OF SENTENCE: The doe and her fawn worked their way along the fence, browsing on the fresh sprouts.

When the phrase is at the end of the sentence, a comma may sometimes be the only indicator of the intended meaning:

Jeff cautiously watched the stranger, trying to guess his next move.

Jeff cautiously watched the stranger trying to guess his next move.

In the first sentence, it is Jeff who is trying to guess the stranger's next move. In the second, it is the stranger who is trying to guess Jeff's.

Finally, we have phrases whose headword is a past participle rather than a present participle. These phrases follow exactly the same pattern you are already familiar with. Restrictive phrases maintain the same voice level without pause and do not require commas:

The museum displayed a manuscript written in A.D. 976.

The recipe calls for one cup of milk mixed with a half-cup of sugar.

Nonrestrictive phrases must be set off with commas:

Senator Murray, urged by his friends and constituents, decided to run again.

The phrase may be shifted to other positions:

> Urged by his friends and constituents, Senator Murray decided to run again.
> Senator Murray decided to run again, urged by his friends and constituents.

Self-Test

The following sentences include various kinds of verbal phrases, some requiring commas and some not. Place commas only where they are needed.

1. Trying to descend the ice-covered steps she fell wrenching her left shoulder.
2. The speaker continued showing color slides of his trip across central Australia.
3. Terrorized by a gun-wielding Central American the pilot changed his course from Miami to Havana.
4. Thousands of frogs trilled in the wet meadows brought out by the sudden spring warmth.
5. To find a cure for cancer we must first discover its cause.
6. Understanding a woman is man's greatest challenge.
7. To expect nothing is worse than to expect too much.

(Answers on p. 81.)

20. HOW TO USE COMMAS WITH INTERRUPTIVE WORDS OR WORD GROUPS

You already know one kind of interruptive expression—the transitional word or phrase which helps carry a thought from one sentence to the next (sections 11 and 12, pp. 20–22). Such words or word groups are called "interruptive" because they are not an integral part of the grammatical structure of the sentence. They are not *grammatically* connected with any particular word, but fit loosely into any position where they create the least interference with the normal flow of the sentence.

> On the other hand, most people find such rigid routines boring.
> ALTERNATIVE: Most people, on the other hand, find such rigid routines boring.

Interruptive expressions are classed as "sentence modifiers," because they relate to the meaning of the sentence as a whole. This difference can be easily grasped in the following examples. In the first sentence, the phrase "without doubt" is grammatically tied to another element in the sentence:

> He can now face the future without doubt.

The phrase "without doubt" modifies the verb "can face." The sentence clearly means that the subject "he" can be free of doubt in facing the future.

But in the following sentence, the same phrase no longer modifies the verb:

> Without doubt, he can now face the future.

"Without doubt" modifies the sentence as a whole, and is clearly an expression of opinion by the writer. It has no specific grammatical connection with any word in the sentence, and can be shifted in position.

> He can, without doubt, now face the future.
> He can now, without doubt, face the future.

Commas are necessary to set such interruptive expressions apart from the rest of the sentence. Otherwise, they might accidentally appear to form a grammatical connection that is not intended. Furthermore, interruptive expressions are usually accompanied by a pause and change in voice level, and the commas coincide with these points.

Sentence modifiers are often single words:

> The hawk, unhappily, was killed.

20. Commas and interrupters

> The fuel was exhausted, apparently, before the plane could reach the base.
>
> Some people, unfortunately, do not see a doctor at the first signs of serious illness.
>
> Obviously, the same person cannot be in two places at the same time.

The commas may sometimes be safely omitted, but only when the interruption seems slight and the meaning is not affected:

> The same person obviously cannot be in two places at the same time.
>
> The fuel apparently was exhausted before the plane could reach the base.

Notice, however, the importance of the comma in the following sentences:

> George walked out of the meeting unhappily.
>
> George walked out of the meeting, unhappily.

In the first example, it is George who is unhappy; in the second, it is the writer. Always set off the sentence modifier with commas if there is any possibility of confusion.

But if the sentence modifier is a word group rather than a single word, commas are almost invariably necessary:

> To tell the truth, we did not expect a favorable response.
>
> All things considered, the democratic system of government is as efficient as any other.
>
> The interior of a spacecraft, to be sure, is not as comfortable as a living room.

Dependent clauses and even short independent sentences may be inserted as interrupters. These must always be set off with commas:

> The two deaths, as I have explained, can both be traced to a faulty ventilating system.
>
> In case you are interested, the winning numbers are posted every Monday in grocery stores.

46 • Standard Prose Sentences

Could anyone in the country, I wonder, command such a sound English style today?

This condition, it seems, is difficult to attain without a special diet and frequent fasting.

What, we ask, was the life of an ordinary man or woman like in the time of Shakespeare?

21. HOW TO USE PAIRS OF DASHES

A pair of dashes sets apart a word or word group more forcefully than commas are able to do. Dashes should therefore be used only where commas are not suitable, and not indiscriminately as a substitute for them. Dashes indicate that the sentence is suspended while some remark is being inserted as an illustration, enlargement, or clarification:

No doubt they are brave—no one will deny that—but bravery is partly an affair of the nerves.

This interruptive word group is not a sentence modifier, but a completely independent sentence inserted in the middle of another one.

A pair of dashes allows you to bring in illustrative examples with naturalness and ease, that would be laborious if handled more formally:

Thus to go from one great novelist to another—from Jane Austen to Hardy, from Peacock to Trollope, from Scott to Meredith—is to be wrenched and uprooted.

The dashes in this example are not substitutes for commas. This can be readily seen if the dashes are replaced with commas:

Thus to go from one great novelist to another, from Jane Austen to Hardy, from Peacock to Trollope, from Scott to Meredith, is to be wrenched and uprooted.

The sentence reads like a continuous series rather than a group of examples which illustrate and enlarge on the opening statement. A pair of dashes is needed to separate the examples from the rest of the sentence.

Even though dashes are not simply a substitute for commas, they may occasionally be used in place of commas to set apart clauses or phrases that have the force of illustration or enlargement:

> When she felt that she had been relieved of the last of her family obligations—though her hair was now turning gray—she came on to New York City and lived there alone for years, occupying herself with the theater, reading, visits to her nephews and nieces—with whom she was extremely popular—and all the spectacle and news of the larger world which she had always loved so much but from which she had spent most of her life removed.

This eighty-one-word sentence is a complicated structure of phrases and clauses which the writer has skillfully rendered more readable and clear by enclosing two of the clauses between pairs of dashes. But notice that both clauses lend themselves naturally to this treatment. They contribute information that simply enlarges on the more basic ideas of the rest of the sentence. Both could be omitted without damaging either the grammatical structure or the meaning.

Do not combine a comma with a dash. The dash eliminates the need for a comma by standing in its place.

Notice that this section concerns only the use of a *pair* of dashes to enclose an inserted expression. The single dash will be treated in Section 23, p. 51.

22. HOW TO USE PARENTHESES

Parentheses are used only in pairs—never singly. Their sole purpose is to enclose words or word groups which stand completely outside the sentence pattern. They are like "asides":

48 • Standard Prose Sentences

He talked at great length about his favorite novelist (Faulkner) and about his favorite motion-picture director (Mike Nichols).

The slow movement of his Fourth Piano Concerto (the dialogue between piano and orchestra) reminds me of the dialogue between Orpheus and the Furies in Gluck.

Once upon a time (this is an anecdote) I went for a week's holiday on the Continent with an Indian friend.

The parentheses do not replace any other punctuation. They simply enclose material that stands outside the sentence pattern. All other punctuation marks normally required in the sentence must still be used in their regular places:

Why, I ask (not of course on the wireless), are you so damnably modest?

Without its parenthetical interruption, the sentence reads:

Why, I ask, are you so damnably modest?

A pair of commas encloses the intrusive expression "I ask." The parenthetical remark is inserted as a part of that expression, and therefore must also fall within the commas. The commas enclose the entire word group:

I ask (not of course on the wireless)

Do not place commas in conjunction with parentheses unless the basic sentence pattern requires them.

COMMAS NOT REQUIRED: The slow movement of his Fourth Piano Concerto (the dialogue between piano and orchestra) reminds me of the dialogue between Orpheus and the Furies in Gluck.

Here, the parenthetical expression falls between a subject and its verb. A comma is not called for by the basic sentence pattern:

The slow movement of his Fourth Piano Concerto reminds me of the dialogue between Orpheus and the Furies in Gluck.

22. Parentheses • 49

The parenthetical element is inserted with no additional punctuation.

The material *within* the parentheses may require its own internal punctuation. This is determined solely by the grammatical structure of the parenthetical expression itself:

> The more expensive Persian rugs contain seven or eight hundred knots per square inch (some even have a thousand, although this is unusual), while the cheaper ones are more loosely woven.

In the example above, the parenthetical material happens to be a complete sentence:

> Some even have a thousand, although this is unusual.

But notice that when this sentence is placed inside parentheses and inserted into the middle of another sentence as an interruptive remark, it loses both its initial capital letter and its period at the end. Only its *internal* punctuation—a comma—is retained.

> WRONG: The more expensive Persian rugs contain seven or eight hundred knots per square inch (Some even have a thousand, although this is unusual.), while the cheaper ones are more loosely woven. [Change the capital letter to lower case, and omit the period after "unusual."]

But question marks or exclamation points may be retained:

> She had a habit of casually dropping names of prominent people (such as Jacqueline Onassis, Truman Capote, or Lauren Bacall—and who doesn't know who *they* are!) as if they were personal friends.

A complete and separate sentence may be independently enclosed within parentheses:

> The writers whom Nabokov has translated into three languages are, with few exceptions, artists of the first rank. (As a very young man he translated Romain Rolland, which is somewhat amusing in view of his comments about Rolland in more recent years.)

50 • Standard Prose Sentences

In such cases, the final parenthesis is placed *after* the period at the end of the sentence. The entire sentence, including its end punctuation, goes inside the parentheses, since it is not inserted within the context of another sentence. But when the parenthetical material occupies just a part of the sentence, the period is placed outside the parenthesis:

> The more expensive Persian rugs contain seven or eight hundred knots per square inch (some even have a thousand, although this is unusual).

The rule is simple: When a parenthesis occurs at the end of a sentence, place the period inside only if the entire sentence is enclosed in parentheses. Place the period outside if just a part of the sentence is so enclosed.

There is no fixed limit to the length of the material that can be enclosed within a single pair of parentheses. Not only entire sentences but even a group of two, three, or more may be set apart within parentheses if there is a suitable reason for doing so. In his novel *Absalom, Absalom!* William Faulkner employed parentheses frequently to enclose explanatory "asides," at least one of which runs to a full page and includes two long paragraphs. But this case is extreme, governed by the imaginative purposes of the novelist. In standard nonfiction prose, parenthetical material is ordinarily brief, so that the reader will not lose the interrupted train of thought.

Self-Test

The following sentences all contain interruptive expressions. Some require commas, some require pairs of dashes, and some require parentheses. Insert the punctuation that seems most suitable in each case.

1. The President it appears was not given the facts by his own generals.
2. The flying saucer descended to the level of the treetops if one can believe the witness, who is not known to be

reliable and emitted several beams of brilliant bluish light.
3. In 1949 this was three years after his escape Walter Bannon was reported working at a gasoline station in southern Ohio.
4. The vehicle was listed as "inoperative" translated into ordinary English, that means smashed beyond repair.
5. Did President Johnson as you see it have the right to enlarge the war without congressional approval?
6. The North Koreans insisted on their right to control international waters a very debatable point, to be sure and threatened to attack any other vessels approaching their shores.

(Answers on p. 81.)

23. HOW TO USE THE SINGLE DASH

Manuals of punctuation usually surround the dash with an air of caution and disapproval, as if its use had certain inherent dangers, like alcohol or gunpowder, and the unskilled were likely to go afoul in using it. It is said to be rather informal and hence not always appropriate to a formal style. It is also criticized as a too-easy substitute for other marks such as the comma and semicolon, suggesting lazy and careless writing. Neither charge is justified.

In spite of the conservative tradition of disapproval of the dash, it is recognized by experienced writers as a versatile and indispensable mark which conveys certain shades of meaning better than any other. It has regularly been used for over two centuries by many of the best English stylists, in both formal and informal usage.

The special meaning of the dash can be grasped more readily than that of most other punctuation marks, eliminating the danger that it may be used indiscriminately as an improper substitute for supposedly better punctuation. More than any other mark, it gives force, flexibility, interest, and variety.

As long ago as 1848, Edgar Allan Poe complained that "every writer for the press, who has any sense of the accurate, must have been frequently mortified and vexed at the distortion of his sentences by the printer's now general substitution of a semi-colon, or comma, for the dash of the manuscript." The dash, he said, represents "a second thought — an emendation. In using it just above I have exemplified its use." After writing the words "a second thought," he continued:

> I reflected whether it would not be possible to render their meaning more distinct by certain other words. Now, instead of erasing the phrase "a second thought," which is of some *use* — which *partially* conveys the idea intended — which advances me *a step toward* my full purpose — I suffer it to remain, and merely put a dash between it and the phrase "an emendation." The dash gives the reader a choice between two, or among three or more expressions, one of which may be more forcible than another, but all of which help out the idea. It stands, in general, for these words — "or, to make my meaning more distinct." This force *it has* — and this force no other point can have; since all other points have well-understood uses quite different from this. Therefore, the dash *cannot* be dispensed with.

The dash breaks the sentence and suspends the reader's attention momentarily, signaling that the following words are an illustration, example, explanation, or enlargement of what went before.

The English novelist E. M. Forster uses the dash freely in his essay "Notes on the English Character":

> There is one more consideration — a most important one.
>
> For it is not that the Englishman can't feel — it is that he is afraid to feel. He has been taught at his public school that feeling is bad form. He must not express great joy or sorrow, or even open his mouth too wide as he talks — his pipe might fall out if he did.

The following example is from Edmund Wilson's essay "A. E. Housman":

> It was a queer destiny, and one that cramped him — if one should not say rather that he had cramped himself.

And from Virginia Woolf's "How Should One Read A Book?":

It may be one letter—but what a vision it gives!
It may be a few sentences—but what vistas they suggest!

These three writers are widely regarded as masters of modern English style, and all use the dash freely. Their style has been called "informal" because of its air of easy naturalness. But it is not "informal" in the sense of a personal letter or a note to the milkman. In its artfulness, careful control, and depth of thought, it is indeed formal. The dash is rarely out of place in any kind of style, any more than is the comma or period.

It is true that in each of the above examples some other punctuation could be substituted:

There is one more consideration, a most important one.

The comma, however, turns the last phrase into a simple appositive, and as such it loses its whole force and importance as an enlargement upon the sentence idea.

Forster could also have correctly used a semicolon in another sentence:

For it is not that the Englishman can't feel; it is that he is afraid to feel.

But the semicolon merely shows a connection, whereas the dash emphasizes the second clause as an enlargement and explanation of the first. The fact that the writer is able to choose between two alternative punctuation marks does not mean that they are identical. He is really choosing between two shades of meaning.

The expression that follows a single dash must obviously come at the end of a sentence, since it is, as Poe said, a "second thought." When such expressions are placed in the middle of the sentence, they must be set off with a *pair* of dashes, as you have already seen above in Section 21. This sentence from George Orwell's "Politics and the English Language" demonstrates:

Political language — and with variations this is true of all political parties, from Conservatives to Anarchists — is designed to make lies sound truthful and murder respectable, and to give an appearance of solidity to pure wind.

A pair of dashes, like a single dash, implies that the enclosed expression is an explanatory enlargement to be given special force and emphasis. Parentheses, on the other hand, imply an "aside":

So (as the voice says) man dreams on.

The following sentence by Edmund Wilson is a fine example of how both dashes and parentheses can be used to draw careful distinctions:

Have those classical scholars who write history, who write criticism, who make translations — Gibbon and Renan and Verrall and Murray and Jowett and Mackail (to take in the whole field of the classics) — no excuse for existing, then?

The dash appears to be gaining rapidly in popularity. In a recent one-page article on the origin of the moon, single dashes are used twice and pairs of dashes four times. In one instance, two pairs of dashes are used in a single sentence:

Astronomers believe it possible that a large primitive planet may somehow have become elongated, and then split into two planets — earth and Mars — leaving a small amount of planetary material — the moon — in between them.

The instant clarity created by the dash is highly attractive in an age of mass-produced printed materials. It allows important illustrative or explanatory matter to stand out in bold relief, actually increasing the reader's speed of comprehension. In an earlier time, commas would have been used to set off the appositives in the above example rather than dashes. But commas are slower paced, less forceful, and since they have several different functions, are likely to be less immediately clear, especially when other unavoidable commas occur in the same sentence.

The dash may also be used somewhat more freely to create dramatic suspense leading up to a contrast or an important conclusion:

23. Single dash • 55

The possibility that the astronauts will actually bring back with them any bacteria which could multiply to epidemic proportions on earth is minute—but it does exist.

The rocks they bring home may provide clues to the origin of the moon, the earth, and even the solar system—and set the course for future expeditions to probe the universe beyond present imagination.

The dash has one additional use: to indicate a break or sudden change in spoken conversation:

"No—but your whole attitude toward emotion is wrong."
"Well, I was going to—I was going to steal it if I had to."

The dash is not recognized by manufacturers of typewriters. The customary way to indicate a dash in typing is to place two hyphens side by side (--).

24. HOW TO USE THE COLON

The first thing to learn about the colon is that it is not related to the semicolon, in spite of its name. Each mark has its own distinctly separate and different uses.

The colon has more in common with the single dash. It anticipates, or announces, something to follow. Its simplest function is merely to introduce a list of items:

Each student must bring the following: pillow, blanket, bed linens, and study lamp.

The Declaration of Independence asserts three basic rights: life, liberty, and the pursuit of happiness.

Grammatically, such itemized lists are in apposition with the last word preceding the colon ("The following," and "rights"). Do *not* use a colon before such lists when they are simply objects of a verb or preposition.

WRONG: Each student must bring: a pillow, blankets, bed linens, and a study lamp. [Omit the colon.]

WRONG: The Declaration of Independence asserted the right to: life, liberty, and the pursuit of happiness. [Omit the colon.]

The introductory sentence may lead up to only a single word, as well as to a series or list of items:

The American people crave one thing above all: peace.

Or it may introduce a word group:

The American people crave one thing above all: an end to the war.

Or even another complete sentence:

Einstein's theory was tested by a simple observation: The light-rays from Mercury appeared to bend as they passed the sun in a direct line to the earth.

When a complete sentence follows the colon, the first word is capitalized by many writers (as in the above example). However, a small letter is equally correct:

This particular attitude reveals such insensitiveness as to suggest a more serious charge: is the Englishman altogether indifferent to the things of the spirit?

In all these examples, the colon simply means "as follows." The reader expects a definition, a more detailed statement, or even a restatement. It is therefore more limited and specialized than the dash, which can set off almost any explanatory or illustrative material that requires emphasis.

The colon may be used following a date or place name, as in a diary. Edmund Wilson employs it in his essay "Miami":

Cotton Blossom Express: I went to sleep in the winter darkness, and wake up to a dazzle of golden light on green palms and low-growing pines that drip with Florida moss.

Miami: I have never been here before and am astounded by this place.

Finally, we come to a somewhat subtler use of the colon as a mark that announces or introduces. It can stand between two sentences, the second of which enlarges upon the first, explains it more fully, or adds specific detail to illustrate:

> We know what the sea looks like from a distance: it is of one color, and level, and obviously cannot contain such creatures as fish.
>
> It was built at the end of the eighteenth century: the first event recorded in connection with it is a memorial service for General Washington.

It can also introduce an antithesis (or opposing idea) that contrasts with the first:

> He did not "borrow" the money: he stole it.
> The president says yes: the people say no.

A somewhat outmoded use of the colon is simply to balance two equal statements:

> The war must be won: the peace must be preserved.

Self-Test

Place a single dash or colon in the appropriate place in each of the following sentences.

1. December 7, 1941 The day dawned peacefully over an unsuspecting Pearl Harbor.
2. They pleaded for help you refused it.
3. That's exactly what it is a lie.
4. The sky turned almost black a threatening, foreboding greenish-black.
5. He turned his face it was bleeding.
6. They demanded three things equal representation, a right to vote, and the right to police themselves.

(Answers on p. 82.)

25. HOW TO END A SENTENCE

Up to this point, all the punctuation marks discussed have been *internal;* that is, they indicate division or connections within a sentence, and are never placed at the end.

End punctuation is simple. There are only three possible marks: period (.), question mark (?), and exclamation point (!).

> You are leaving.
> Are you leaving?
> You're leaving!

If all sentences were as obvious as these, there would never be a problem. But a very troublesome problem often annoys the struggling writer: where, exactly, is the end of the sentence? Students often have papers returned to them with sentences marked "Fragment." That is, they have treated an incomplete or fragmentary part of a sentence as if it were the whole thing.

> WRONG: The president condemned the student protest movement. Although he should have known better.

Why is this wrong? By now, you may recognize that the second part is a dependent clause which cannot stand by itself. Both parts should be combined in a single sentence with a comma between them:

> The president condemned the student movement, although he should have known better.

An incorrect sentence fragment is a split-off word group which grammatically and logically belongs with some base sentence. Usually such fragments *follow* the base sentence. Very rarely does anyone make a fragment out of a phrase or clause at the beginning of a sentence.

> UNLIKELY TO OCCUR: Although he should have known better. The president condemned the student protest movement.

25. End punctuation • 59

Almost any kind of phrase or clause occurring at the end of the sentence may accidentally be chopped off by a period and turned into a fragment.

> WRONG: The curtains were a brilliant red-violet. A color I detest. [Appositive.]
> RIGHT: The curtains were a brilliant red-violet, a color I detest.
> WRONG: The scoutmaster told them several stories. Which they didn't believe. [Adjective clause.]
> RIGHT: The scoutmaster told them several stories, which they didn't believe.

Linguistic scientists have shown that the voice always drops to the lowest pitch level when it arrives at the end of a declarative sentence. This drop in pitch is indicated in writing by a period. If the fragments shown as examples above were read aloud, it would be obvious that the period does *not* stand for the true and intended end of the sentence. The voice may drop slightly to indicate a pause and an internal separation, but it does not drop to the lowest level that the end of a sentence demands. Sentence fragments can always be recognized by the fact that the period forces an unnatural voice-drop where none belongs. This rule can be clearly illustrated:

> RIGHT: He ran into the house.
> WRONG: He ran. Into the house.

Even the poorest writer would be unlikely to split such a sentence in two. But long sentences with subordinate clauses, appositives, or long phrases at the end are sometimes split in two just as improperly, in exactly the same way. Incorrect fragments, then, are amputated word groups that belong grammatically to a preceding sentence.

In contrast, certain kinds of word groups *can* sometimes stand alone even though they are not grammatically complete sentences in themselves. But they are *not* amputated fragments of a sentence that ought to be kept whole:

60 • Standard Prose Sentences

> You can stay away a long time. Forever, in fact.

The second part of this example is not a fragment, but rather a condensed sentence in its own right. It can be expanded to read:

> You can stay away forever, in fact.

Legitimately incomplete sentences are ordinarily nothing more than such elliptical, or shortened and condensed, sentences.

> The warm sympathy, the romance, the imagination, that we look for in Englishmen whom we meet, and too often vainly look for, must exist in the nation as a whole, or we could not have this outburst of national song. An undeveloped heart, not a cold one.
> Do we mean unconscious deceit? Muddle-headedness?

Such word groups should not be called fragments, even though they do not have a subject and a verb. They are simply condensed sentences that depend on a preceding sentence to supply the full meaning.

Spoken conversation is normally composed of many such elliptical statements:

> "I'm going in to town tomorrow."
> "When?"
> "Oh, fairly early."
> "Before eight?"
> "No, no, not before nine-thirty."

Notice that each word group has the same voice pattern that a complete sentence would have. This kind of incomplete sentence is perfectly legitimate in writing as well as in speaking, whenever it helps to avoid repetition or add emphasis.

Sentences may properly begin with "and" or "but." Remember that these are not subordinating conjunctions: they do not introduce a dependent word group.

The French withdrew after failing to maintain order, and a long series of upheavals finally resulted in a new government. But that is another story.

The question mark is never used when a question is worded indirectly as a declarative statement:

> DECLARATIVE STATEMENT: He asked what had happened to our liberties.
> QUESTION: What has happened to our liberties?

Self-Test

Identify improper fragments, and connect them with their preceding sentences. Leave legitimately incomplete word groups as they are.

1. The United States purchased Alaska from Russia. For a very low price.
2. Do you want to risk nuclear retaliation? Mass extermination of the populace?
3. He loved the sound of the old clocks. Ticking in the quiet afternoon. Chiming in the night.
4. Losses amounted to $63,743 in a single year. And that does not include the cost of damage done to property.
5. Some citizens realize the value of public education and do not object to paying school taxes. Even though they have no children of their own.
6. First, a word about the Extension Service.

(Answers on p. 82.)

26. HOW TO QUOTE FROM ANOTHER AUTHOR'S WORK

Quotation marks (" ") always come in pairs. They mark the precise beginning and end of material written or spoken by someone else.

QUOTING AN ENTIRE SENTENCE OR PARAGRAPH

If a complete sentence is quoted, the marks are simply placed around all of it, including its end punctuation:

"Call me Ishmael." These arresting words begin what is perhaps America's greatest novel.

If more than one paragraph is quoted, quotation marks are placed at the beginning of each paragraph but at the end of only the last one:

"When we got the report at ATIC, our first reaction was that the master sergeants had seen a large meteor. From the evidence, I had written off as meteors all previous similar UFO reports from this air base.

"The sergeants' report, however, contained one bit of information that completely changed the previous picture. At the time of the sighting there had been a solid 6,000-foot-thick overcast at 4,700 feet. And meteors don't go that low.

"A few quick calculations gave a rather fantastic answer. If the object was just at the base of the clouds it would have been 10,000 feet from the two observers and traveling 1,400 miles per hour."

Note that no quotation marks are used at the ends of the first two paragraphs. This omission indicates that the quotation has not been completed, but continues into the next paragraph. Quotation marks are used at the *beginning* of each paragraph for the same reason: to show that the quotation continues. Only when the end is reached do marks close the quotation.

One danger, however, in quoting lengthy passages is that they tend to merge with the rest of the text and do not stand out clearly as material by another writer. This problem can be remedied by placing the quoted passage in block form. That is, it is indented on both sides and separated from the rest of the material on the page:

> In another second the three deltas made a slight left bank and shot by the B-25 at terrific speed. The colonels estimated that the speed was at least three times that of an F-86. They got a good look at the three deltas as the unusual craft passed within 400 to 800 yards of the B-25.

When using block form, *omit quotation marks*. They are not necessary, since the block form itself indicates a quotation. In typing, single-space the quoted material.[1] A standard rule is to place anything in block form that is more than five typed lines long.

INTRODUCING A QUOTATION

An introductory statement is often used preceding a quotation. Such a statement may be followed by either a colon or a comma:

> At the inquest, Clifford Barnes stated: "She telephoned me at 1:35 a.m. to say she was afraid to be alone in the house."
>
> At the inquest, Clifford Barnes stated, "She telephoned me at 1:35 a.m. to say she was afraid to be alone in the house."

INDIRECT QUOTATIONS

Do not place quotation marks around *indirect* quotations. These are statements not directly quoted from the writer or speaker, but only referred to:

> At the inquest, Clifford Barnes stated that she telephoned him at 1:35 a.m. to say she was afraid to be alone in the house.

---

[1] Possible exception: If you are typing a manuscript for a publisher or printer, he is likely to prefer that you double-space such quoted material, since he may want to write interlinear directions to the typesetter.

INCORPORATING QUOTED MATERIAL INTO A SENTENCE

Often only a few words or a portion of a sentence are quoted. They must be worked into the sentence pattern as if they were a part of it. Do not place a comma before such quoted fragments incorporated into a larger sentence unless your sentence structure demands it:

> Clifford Barnes claimed that she telephoned him after midnight because she was "afraid to be alone in the house."
> George Orwell says that "every such phrase anaesthetizes a portion of one's brain," and proceeds to demonstrate how eliminating such phrases leads to clearer thinking.

Commas and periods at the end of quoted material always go *inside* the quotation marks. (See the two examples above.) Colons, semicolons, and dashes go *outside:*

> George Orwell says that "every such phrase anaesthetizes a portion of one's brain"; but he does not realize that language cannot be totally free of ready-made phrases.
> George Orwell says that "every such phrase anaesthetizes a portion of one's brain": but who is to draw the line between useful and harmful ready-made phrases?
> George Orwell says that "every such phrase anaesthetizes a portion of one's brain"—a claim that is certain to be argued by extremists of both left and right.

This rule of punctuation has arbitrarily become a convention, though there is no logical reason why periods and commas should be treated differently from other marks. British usage, in fact, does treat them all alike. This convention explains why you have probably sometimes seen commas and periods outside quotation marks. But standard American practice continues to treat them differently.

Question marks and exclamation points go inside quotation marks if they are part of the quotation, outside if they are not:

They are asking, "When will the war end?" [The basic sentence is a statement; the question mark goes not with the basic sentence, but with the question within quotation marks.]

Is this the man they called a "traitor"? [The basic sentence is a question; the quoted word is not. Hence, the question mark goes with the basic sentence, outside the quotation marks.]

The crowd panicked at the shouts of "Fire, fire!"

It is indeed ironic that the discarded portion is an oration against studying "style"!

A quoted question or exclamation may be inserted in the middle of a sentence:

The shout of "Fire!" rang through the crowded auditorium.

The question "Why did it happen?" troubles all Americans.

BREAKING A QUOTATION INTO TWO PARTS

The introductory statement, which attributes the quotation to a given speaker or writer, may also be placed in the middle rather than at the beginning:

"But if thought corrupts language," George Orwell writes, "language can also corrupt thought."

Each half of the quotation must be enclosed by a separate set of quotation marks. The nonquoted material in between is set off by a pair of commas. The first comma *always* goes inside the quotation marks. The second half of the quotation never begins with a capital letter unless the word in the original quotation is capitalized.

The punctuation of the original must always be preserved exactly as it was written. This necessity may present a problem when you wish to break the quotation at some internal punctuation mark in the original such as a comma, colon, dash, or semicolon.

The comma always stays where it is in the original, and remains inside the quotation marks:

"But if thought corrupts language, language can also corrupt thought."

"But if thought corrupts language," George Orwell writes, "language can also corrupt thought."

The colon, semicolon, and dash do *not* stay inside the quotation marks. Instead, they are shifted to the end of the interruptive material, and a comma is inserted inside the quotation marks:

"We know what the sea looks like from a distance: it is of one color, and level, and obviously cannot contain such creatures as fish."

"We know what the sea looks like from a distance," E. M. Forster writes: "it is of one color, and level, and obviously cannot contain such creatures as fish."

"None denies that the corporation could make higher returns by raising prices; the policy rests firmly on the fact that they do not maximize returns."

"None denies that the corporation could make higher returns by raising prices," Galbraith notes; "the policy rests firmly on the fact that they do not maximize returns."

"For it is not that the Englishman can't feel—it is that he is afraid to feel."

"For it is not that the Englishman can't feel," Forster believes—"it is that he is afraid to feel."

INSERTING A BREAK BETWEEN TWO QUOTED SENTENCES

The same pattern is followed when placing the period that separates two complete sentences. That is, the period fol-

26. Quoting • 67

lows the interruptive material when the break comes after a complete sentence:

> "But if thought corrupts language, language can also corrupt thought. A bad usage can spread by tradition and imitation, even among people who should and do know better."
>
> "But if thought corrupts language, language can also corrupt thought," Orwell argues. "A bad usage can spread by tradition and imitation, even among people who should and do know better."

Never place the period inside the quotation marks unless it comes at the end of the entire sentence.

> WRONG: "But if thought corrupts language, language can also corrupt thought." Orwell argues.

The words "Orwell argues" are a continuous part of the sentence. Hence, a comma must be used at the end of the quotation, and the period must be shifted to the end.

The question mark and exclamation point, however, remain inside the quotation marks if they are part of the original quotation:

> "How long must the war last?" they ask us.
> "This way out!" he shouted.

Note: Only *one* punctuation mark is ever used in conjunction with the end-quotation marks. If you use a question mark or exclamation point (as in the examples above), do not use a comma also.

> WRONG: "How long must the war last?", they ask us.

INDICATING THE OMISSION OF WORDS FROM A QUOTATION

A row of three periods (...), called *points of ellipsis*, indicates that one or more words have been omitted from the quoted material.

> COMPLETE QUOTATION: "The principles of social structure and change, if the generalizations of his system were valid, must be the same as those of the universe at large."
>
> WITH ELLIPSIS: "The principles of social structure and change...must be the same as those of the universe at large."

An omitted portion is assumed to be irrelevant to the purpose of the quotation. But the omission must be honestly indicated, since the prime rule is to respect the words of the author or speaker exactly as he expressed them.

A row of four periods, rather than three, is used when the omitted portion comes at the end of a quoted sentence rather than in the middle of it. Three periods indicate the omission, while the fourth stands for the end of the sentence.

> COMPLETE QUOTATION: "The conversion of the scientists promised early success in the universities, where the atmosphere was charged with electricity."
>
> WITH ELLIPSIS: "The conversion of the scientists promised early success in the universities...."

Points of ellipsis are used only to show omissions in material that is otherwise continuous in the original. When drawing together words or phrases that are widely scattered over a number of pages in the original text, do not put them all within one set of quotation marks, using points of ellipsis to show the large spaces between. Instead, place each quotation within a separate set of quotation marks, even if you blend them into a single sentence:

> According to E. M. Forster, the English character is "slow," "incomplete," and guilty of "unconscious deceit," but lacking in "treachery, cruelty, and fanaticism."

This construction permits you to reorganize and summarize another writer's ideas while singling out important words and phrases.

INSERTING EDITORIAL COMMENT WITHIN A QUOTATION

The rule of honesty requires that you make no changes, corrections, or additions in another writer's words unless you make clear that you are doing so. But sometimes a quotation contains a misspelling, a historical inaccuracy, or incomplete information which you wish to point out. In such cases you may insert an enlargement or correction enclosed in square brackets:

"There is a spurious biography of Edgar A. Poe [by Rufus Griswold] which has been extensively published in newspapers and magazines."

"William Ellery Channing is, I believe, the son [actually, the nephew] of the great sermonizer of that same name."

Brackets are occasionally necessary in the editing of hastily written manuscripts such as letters or diaries, where slips are likely to occur, and omitted words or portions of words must be filled in to make sense. These examples from Thoreau's journal demonstrate:

"Remote[nes]s throws all sound into my inmost being...."

"Our task is not such a piece of day labor that a [man] must be thinking what he shall do next for a livelihood...."

Incorrect or unusual spellings, incorrect usage, or coined words, may surprise the reader and make him suspect that the quotation is not accurate. The word *sic* (Latin, meaning *thus* or *so*) may be inserted immediately following such words to indicate that they are quoted exactly as in the original:

"I love to consider the silent economy and tidiness of nature, how after all the filfth [sic] of the woods, and the accumulated impurities of the winter have been rinsed herein, this liquid transparency appears in the spring."

Square brackets are not to be confused with parentheses. Their only function is to indicate editorial insertions. Since most typewriters are not equipped with brackets, you will have to draw them in by hand. Never use parentheses as a substitute.

QUOTING WITHIN A QUOTATION

Place single quotation marks around material which is already enclosed in quotation marks in the original text:

> "Yet this was not characteristic of Darwin's moral sentiments, for he went on to say that a ruthless policy of elimination would betray 'the noblest part of our nature,' which is itself securely founded on the social instincts."

Follow the same rules for placing commas and other marks in conjunction with single quotation marks that you observe with regular, or double, quotation marks.

If the quotation-within-a-quotation comes at the end of the sentence, the single and double quotation marks will coincide. Both must still be used, and the period goes inside both:

> "His opponents might conclude from this that 'society is doomed to hopeless degeneracy.'"

Note: Spoken dialogue, as in fiction, is treated in Part III, p. 116.

QUOTING TITLES

Titles of books, plays, long poems, and magazines and other periodicals are italicized. (In manuscript, they are underlined to indicate italicizing.)

Lolita
The Glass Menagerie
Paradise Lost
Esquire
Encyclopaedia Britannica

Because newspapers and some magazines do not have italic type, they frequently enclose all titles in quotation marks or use no indication at all. This practice should be avoided in writing, however, where the distinction between underscoring and quotation marks should be maintained.

Titles of short stories, articles, chapters from books, and shorter poems—in other words, all short works and isolated parts of longer works—are placed within quotation marks.

"Flowering Judas"
"The Obscenity Racket Today"
"Comic Books—Blueprints for Delinquency"
"Ode to Dejection"

Capitalize the first and last words in the title, and all other words except the articles *a, an,* and *the,* conjunctions, and short prepositions.

QUOTING LINES OF POETRY

Poetry may be either quoted in block form and centered on the page separate from the rest of the text, or incorporated into a sentence if the quotation consists of only two or three lines:

> And malt does more than Milton can
> To justify God's ways to man.

According to A. E. Housman, "malt does more than Milton can /To justify God's ways to man."

The diagonal line, or bar, is used to mark the end of a line of poetry when it is incorporated into a prose passage. Note that the first word of the following line is capitalized as in the original.

27. OTHER USES (AND ABUSES) OF QUOTATION MARKS

Although italics are preferred, quotation marks may be used to indicate that a word is being referred to as a word:

> The word "zymurgy" is often the last in a dictionary.
> The word *zymurgy* is often the last in a dictionary.

72 • Standard Prose Sentences

An informal or slang word out of context, or a word used in a precise technical sense, is sometimes placed in quotation marks:

> In the terminology of his peers, he was considered "cool."
> In seeking an answer to this question we shall first go back to the concept of the "symbol," as Heinrich Hertz characterized it from the standpoint of natural science.

However, do not use quotation marks in a self-conscious display of learning, or in an embarrassed attempt to show that you are aware of clichés and trite expressions. (Eliminate such expressions, preferably.)

> POOR: She added just "a wee bit" of garlic salt, and stirred "to beat the band."

Quotation marks are sometimes used, too, to express irony and sarcasm, or to point up a pun. Good writers seldom resort to this usage, while poor ones seem to have a fondness for it. Again, this use of quotation marks is better avoided, but may on rare occasions be helpful:

> Hello, "beautiful."
> Fat people are looking for a "weigh" out of their problems.

Amateur writers of advertisements sometimes imagine that quotation marks are a form of decoration, and place them around words with no sense of propriety or purpose.

> POOR:
> Mr. John,
> "Hairdresser Extraordinaire"
> invites you
> to an
> "Open House"
> Tuesday, October 14, 1:00 to 5:00 p.m.
> to celebrate his
> "Grand Opening"

> The Oyster Shell
> "Where gourmets gather"

In the second example above, the supposed quotation is meant to appear as an endorsement by someone or other. In actual fact, of course, it is a slogan devised by the management. Although this practice has been in vogue for many years, it seems to be on the way out among the more sophisticated copywriters.

28. PUTTING IT ALL TOGETHER

Looking at punctuation now as a whole, we can see that it is an art of expression (as Poe claimed) rather than a set of laws. Punctuation must fit the sentence pattern and thought. Sometimes no one can tell you exactly which mark *must* be used; you must make a few decisions on your own. For example, you might punctuate a portion of the sentence above in at least three different ways:

> We can see that it is an art of expression, as Poe claimed, rather than a set of laws.
> We can see that it is an art of expression — as Poe claimed — rather than a set of laws.
> We can see that it is an art of expression (as Poe claimed) rather than a set of laws.

Which is "best"? It depends on the writer's intention. The phrase "as Poe claimed" is regarded as an intrusive expression. But commas allow it to take on undue importance, as if it were closely integrated with the train of thought. Dashes throw a spotlight on it as if it deserved too much separate emphasis. Parentheses imply that it is an aside. The last alternative seemed right for this particular sentence.

In the same fashion, almost every punctuation mark offers some degree of free choice. A comma may suddenly become necessary to avoid misunderstanding even though customary practice would omit it. For example, a comma is not necessary to divide the following compound sentence:

She is candid with Strether and he realizes his own worth.

But add a phrase, and the sentence is confusing:

She is candid with Strether and with Maria's help, he realizes his own worth.

"And" seems to connect two phrases—"with Strether and with Maria's help." An additional comma clarifies the sentence:

She is candid with Strether, and with Maria's help, he realizes his own worth.

Here are some additional ways in which commas make distinctions.

SHOWING OMISSIONS

A full statement may occasionally require you to repeat words you can better omit. A comma will allow you to telescope the sentence:

In 1967, the Hanford Corporation earned $2,300,000 and Mod Products, $1,125,000.

The comma replaces the verb "earned," which the reader automatically fills in because of the obvious parallelism.

POINTING UP CONTRAST

Negative word groups are frequently set apart with commas even though positive word groups having similar grammatical structure might not be:

I raised the window and looked out.
I looked out, but saw nothing.
The flowers were red and white.
The flowers were red, not white.

SHOWING A RESTATEMENT OR ENLARGEMENT FOR CLARITY

You have already seen that two kinds of word groups which repeat or enlarge upon some other sentence element are set apart with commas:

NONRESTRICTIVE CLAUSE: My brother, who is younger than I am, is already married.

APPOSITIVE: My brother, a young man, is already married.

The same principle applies to another kind of restatement as well:

We can compound, or double, the subject.

The commas here indicate that the words "or double" simply define, or restate, the meaning of "compound."

Without commas, the sentence would imply a choice of alternatives—either one or the other—rather than a repetition:

We can compound or double the subject.

It is a mistake to believe that you can write what you wish and then go back and add the punctuation, as if punctuation marks were only a necessary evil required by printers, editors, and English teachers. Punctuation must be mastered along with writing itself as a part of expressed meaning. In fact, a good grasp of what punctuation can do will actually free you to write with a show of greater intelligence and flexibility. Many an amateur writer has been brought to a helpless standstill by his inability to punctuate the sentences he can think of in his mind. A knowledge of punctuation can help shape a sentence from the beginning, opening up possibilities for easy expression of involved ideas.

For example, Edmund Wilson in writing about Emily Post's *Etiquette* wished to bring in a great deal of quoted material for illustration, including several lines of conversational dialogue:

Bobo Gilding (whose nickname is incidentally explained in a section intended to discourage what Mrs. Post calls conversational "door-slammers": "As for the name 'Bobo,' it's asinine." "Oh, it's just one of those children's names that stick sometimes for life." "Perfect rot. Ought to be called by his name.")—Bobo Gilding, on his side, does not care for his aunt's rather pompous parties, since "entering a drawing-room [for Bobo] was more suggestive of the daily afternoon tea ordeal of his early nursery days than a voluntary act of pleasure."

To be sure, this example shows a rather more complicated mass of material within parentheses than most writers would attempt, and Mr. Wilson is obliged to break a conventional rule by using periods with the parentheses. But he preserves the easy continuous flow of his presentation, and avoids breaking it up into shorter sentences and paragraphs. He is able to frame an illustration within the sentence to which it relates, instead of separating it from the sentence and placing it less logically either before or after.

This chapter of *The Way to Punctuate* has aimed to show that every punctuation mark should have an explainable and justifiable reason, related to the precise meaning you wish to get across to the reader. Punctuation should not be handled blindly any more than should the words of a sentence.

ANSWERS TO SELF-TESTS

Page 8 (Items in series)

1. Norman Mailer is Hemingway's great disciple, rival, admirer, and critic.
2. The frightened snake hissed and struck. [No comma is necessary unless you wish to separate the two verbs for dramatic emphasis: The frightened snake hissed, and struck.]
3. The frightened snake coiled, hissed, and struck.
4. Alice was neither wife, sister, nor mother.
5. Norman Mailer is Hemingway's great disciple and admirer. [Only two items; no comma is needed.]
6. Rain, high winds, and falling temperatures are predicted for the Middle West. [The series of three items is subject

Answers to Self-tests • 77

of the verb "are predicted." No comma should follow "temperatures," since this would separate subject from verb.]
7. Maturity and intelligence are two characteristics of a leader.
8. The village was small, lonely, and isolated.
9. They wasted their time, their effort, their money.
10. Conflicts have occurred between students and faculty, students and administration, and faculty and administration. [This sentence contains a series of three pairs.]

Page 10 (Strings of modifiers)

1. Antonio's grandmother was very short, black-haired, and and extremely thin.
2. Tiny green insects buzzed at the window. [The first three words are like "clear blue sky."]
3. She played with all her little toy animals. [The only true adjective in the string is "little." Since there are not two or more coordinate adjectives, no commas are needed.]
4. Roderick Usher dwelt in an ancient, decaying mansion.
5. It was an expensive cigarette lighter. ["Cigarette lighter" is a compound noun.]
6. Several brilliant yellow autumn leaves lay on the steps. [See number 3 above. "Yellow" is the only adjective here.]

Page 14 (More complicated series)

Building a better community; improved education; better understanding of the free enterprise system; an effective attack on heart ailments, emphysema, alcoholism, or other crippling diseases; participation in the political party of choice; and renewed emphasis on regular religious observances, are all examples of such further goals.

Page 25 (Joining two sentences)

You are to write your own sentences, but the following model may be used to judge your work.

    The Germans retreated across Africa. Meanwhile, the Allies prepared an assault on western France.

The Germans retreated across Africa; meanwhile, the Allies prepared an assault on western France.

Page 25 (Commas and semicolons in compound sentences)
1. They played tennis, they went for afternoon walks, they read novels by the dozen, but time passed with agonizing slowness.
2. Berlin fell and the Third Reich fell with it. *Or*: Berlin fell, and the Third Reich fell with it.
3. Summers in Death Valley are unbelievably hot, but the animal life is remarkably adapted for survival.
4. The climbing party finally reached a broad ledge on the southwest side of the peak; here they could rest and regain strength.
5. The stock market fluctuated according to news of the war; that is, it rose with each victory and dropped with each setback.
6. Rescue parties attempted to enter the mine three times during the night, but poisonous gases or fire drove them back.
7. Red China has indicated its willingness to resume talks; however, the State Department doubts its sincerity.
8. In any case, you must file your income tax by April 15.

Page 29 (Movable phrases)
1. In short, the cost of living is higher than ever.
2. By morning, the rain had stopped. *Or*: By morning the rain had stopped.
3. The cost of living in a large city is higher than ever.
4. The cost of living, in other words, is higher than ever.
5. After several fruitless attempts, the rescue party reached the thirteen men trapped at the 1200-foot level of the mine.
6. The rescue party reached the trapped miners after several fruitless attempts.
7. Police broke through a door at the head of the stairs in the rear of the house.
8. The ship moved cautiously through the fog toward the harbor mouth.

9. This insect can be found in rotting logs, under dead leaves, and beneath stones.

Page 33 (Clauses and other movable elements out of order)
1. Although I disagree with your beliefs, I defend your right to express them.
2. Lydia Merivale wore white gloves whenever she left her house.
3. Whenever she left her house, Lydia Merivale wore white gloves.
5. The enemy inflicted 5,748 casualties in one month, if we are to believe them. [A loosely related clause is usually separated by a comma regardless of its position.]
6. A profusion of wild flowers, purple, yellow, and white, covered the meadow.
7. The eyes in the portrait seemed to follow her, cold and accusing.

Page 37 (Restrictive and nonrestrictive clauses)
1. Poe, who is viewed by many as a Southern writer, was actually a native of Boston. [Nonrestrictive]
2. A Norwegian fishing boat was grounded on the sandbar which lies just outside the entrance to the harbor. [Restrictive: specifies which sandbar among several. If you place a comma after "sandbar," it becomes nonrestrictive: there is only one sandbar, and the "which" clause merely adds information. In this case, correct punctuation is dependent upon the writer's intended meaning.]
3. The package that we sent on November 10 did not arrive until December 3. ["That" clauses are always restrictive; no comma.]
4. The secret was divulged to two newspaper reporters, who promptly spread it across the evening headlines. [Like 2 above, this may be either restrictive or nonrestrictive, depending upon your intended meaning. A comma here makes it nonrestrictive.]
5. The meadows where cows grazed only ten years ago are now covered with suburban homes. [The "where" clause

is restrictive: it singles out certain particular meadows. Conceivably, it could be made nonrestrictive too.]
6. Harry told a joke which she considered offensive. [Restrictive: it was an offensive joke.]
7. Several villages and one large city lie close to the river, which floods on the average of once every twenty-five years. [Nonrestrictive if there is only one river in the context, in which event the clause simply adds information not necessary to identify the river. Omitting the comma would make the clause restrictive and would intimate that more than one river is in the context.]
8. The money that they counted on for the research project was voted down by the legislature. [Remove the comma: a restrictive clause does not take a comma at either beginning or end.]
9. The time when we should have acted is already past. [Remove both commas: this is clearly a restrictive, not a nonrestrictive, clause.]
10. Several mothers whose sons were in the combat zone wrote letters to Senator Blackwell, who promised to investigate the problem. [Remove the comma after "zone," since the clause is restrictive, but add one after "Blackwell," since the following clause is nonrestrictive. That is, each clause in the test sentence is punctuated the reverse of what it should be.]

Page 39 (Appositives)

1. Her mother, the former Madeline Garfield, had inherited a fortune in oil and steel.
2. Nineteen sixty-eight, a year of unprecedented violence, will be recognized as a turning point in American history.
3. A skilled linguist, Miller translated his own works into French.
4. My friend Stanley has a summer job in British Columbia.
5. Many persons will be called on for aid, particularly those who have had specialized training.
6. The governor's first suggestion, to increase revenues by raising student fees, was reluctantly withdrawn.

Answers to Self-tests • 81

Page 43 (Verbal phrases)

1. Trying to descend the ice-covered steps, she fell, wrenching her left shoulder.
2. The speaker continued showing color slides of his trip across central Australia. [As it stands, this sentence means that the speaker had already been showing slides of central Australia and continued doing so. The addition of a comma after "continued" would change the meaning, suggesting that after a break he had turned to a new subject: "The speaker continued, showing color slides of his trip across central Australia."]
3. Terrorized by a gun-wielding Central American, the pilot changed his course from Miami to Havana.
4. Thousands of frogs trilled in the wet meadows, brought out by the sudden spring warmth. [A comma is necessary in order to show that "brought out" modifies "frogs" rather than "meadows."]
5. To find a cure for cancer, we must first discover its cause.
6. Understanding a woman is man's greatest challenge.
7. To expect nothing is worse than to expect too much.

Pages 50-51 (Interruptive expressions)

1. The President, it appears, was not given the facts by his own generals.
2. The flying saucer descended to the level of the treetops (if one can believe the witness, who is not known to be reliable) and emitted several beams of brilliant bluish light. [Dashes could be used, although the inserted comment is an aside, for which parentheses are more appropriate.]
3. In 1949—this was three years after his escape—Walter Bannon was reported working at a gasoline station in southern Ohio. [Parentheses could be used, but this inserted comment is more an informative enlargement than it is an aside.]
4. The vehicle was listed as "inoperative" (translated into ordinary English, that means smashed beyond repair).

82 • Standard Prose Sentences

5. Did President Johnson, as you see it, have the right to enlarge the war without congressional approval?
6. The North Koreans insisted on their right to control international waters—a very debatable point, to be sure—and threatened to attack any other vessels approaching their shores.

Page 57 (Colon and dash)

1. December 7, 1941: The day dawned peacefully over an unsuspecting Pearl Harbor.
2. They pleaded for help: you refused it.
3. That's exactly what it is—a lie.
4. The sky turned almost black—a threatening, foreboding greenish-black.
5. He turned his face: it was bleeding.
6. They demanded three things: equal representation, a right to vote, and the right to police themselves.

Page 61 (Incomplete word groups and fragments)

1. The United States purchased Alaska from Russia for a very low price.
2. Do you want to risk nuclear retaliation? Mass extermination of the populace?
3. He loved the sound of the old clocks ticking in the quiet afternoon, chiming in the night. [Some writers would consider the sentence more imaginative when split apart as in the example.]
4. Losses amounted to $63,743 in a single year. And that does not include the cost of damage done to property. [The two sentences could be combined, with a comma after "year." But the second part would be less emphatic.]
5. Some citizens realize the value of public education and do not object to paying school taxes, even though they have no children of their own. [The dependent clause cannot stand alone—it is definitely an illegitimate fragment.]
6. First, a word about the Extension Service. [A legitimate telescoped sentence.]

PART II

Arbitrary Marks and Usages

A few special marks—and a few usages of the other marks, such as comma or colon—follow rather fixed, conventional rules. When in doubt, you can always look them up quickly. They seldom require you to make choices.

29. THE HYPHEN SEPARATES PARTS OF WORDS

An individual word almost never needs to be divided internally for *expressive* purposes, as a sentence does. But sometimes you are forced to separate a word into parts, either by syllables or individual letters. A hyphen—which is a short dash (-)—is inserted at such divisions.

DIVISION OF A WORD AT THE END OF A LINE

When part of a word at the end of a line must carry over to the next line, follow the practice of a good dictionary in making the division. In most words this practice is to divide the word between syllables—but not in all. Moreover, it is often difficult to decide whether a consonant in a word belongs with a preceding or a following syllable. Consider these three words:

    cast
    caster   cast-er
    castor   cas-tor

You probably cannot hear a difference between anyone's pronunciation of *caster* and his pronunciation of *castor*.

Consider also the words with doubled letters:

    bottle   bot-tle
    occurrence oc-cur-rence

The two letters in each of these three cases represent single sounds; but you separate these pairs of letters at the end of a line.

The only sure way to avoid an error in this kind of problem is to consult the dictionary or remember its practice accurately. Even so, you can expect disagreement among dictionaries, as in

    service
    serv-ice (Random House)
    ser-vice (Webster III)

Newspapers have almost ceased to be concerned about the places where they divide words, in part because their automatic typesetting machinery is hard to control in these matters. Other publications face the same kind of difficulty and many have all but given up the effort to be accurate or rational about dividing words. But they are submitting to mechanical difficulty which does not affect a person writing a paper or an essay.

Even when you know the syllable division, a few additional principles always apply:

1. Always place the hyphen at the end of the line where the division occurs, never at the beginning of the next.

29. Separating parts of words • 85

2. Never hyphenate a word so as to leave standing alone a syllable of only one or two letters. For example, the word *a-bove* consists of two syllables. But rather than leaving the single syllable *a-* standing alone at the end of the line, carry it over to the next and keep the word in one piece. Similarly, the word *love-ly* should be placed entirely on one line or the other. It is not necessary to save space by carrying over a two-letter syllable, since the hyphen occupies one full space anyway, and one additional space would allow you to complete the word without dividing it.

3. Never divide a single-syllable word, no matter how long it is:

    strength
    wrench
    stopped

4. If you are preparing a manuscript for publication, try to avoid dividing *any* word at the end of a line, even if it means a somewhat ragged margin. This practice is a help to editors and typesetters. Furthermore, a hyphenated word at the end of a line may coincidentally be a compound word, in which the hyphen should be retained even when the entire word is printed on a single line. The typesetter will have no way of knowing whether you intend the hyphen to be retained or dropped. Either might be correct:

    Christ-like
    Christlike

5. Never divide numbers (when written with numerals), the names of organizations abbreviated as a series of capital letters, or any other words similarly composed of a series of capital letters:

    12,712,831
    NAACP
    UNICEF

SEPARATE INDIVIDUAL LETTERS WITH A HYPHEN TO INDICATE SPELLING

EXAMPLE: The prefix of *perspire* is spelled *p-e-r*, not *p-r-e*.

SEPARATE INDIVIDUAL LETTERS TO INDICATE STUTTERING

This point is included in all manuals of punctuation, but the writer should be advised to represent stuttering *only* if it sounds absolutely natural when read aloud. The repetition of sounds is likely to seem contrived and artificial to the reader. If you wish to depict habitual stuttering, it would be wise to make a study of it beforehand in order to acquaint yourself with the speech patterns that actually occur. You will discover, for example, that a stutterer seldom repeats an initial sound in machine-gun fashion ("d-d-don't") but rather locks onto it and is unable to proceed beyond it ("mmmmother"). This kind of sound is virtually impossible to put down accurately on paper. In general, stuttering is best avoided in writing, even though it is conventionally represented by repeating initial letters and connecting them with hyphens.

30. THE HYPHEN JOINS THE PARTS OF SOME COMPOUND WORDS

A compound word is one which consists of two or more normally independent words:

| broad jump | top-heavy | toothpaste |
| living room | baby-sitter | cornmeal |

Compound words appear in three styles, as these examples show: open, hyphenated, and solid.

Generally speaking, the hyphen is used in compounds much less often than either the solid or open form, and the trend in recent years has been increasingly in that direction. You will be safer when in doubt to select either the solid or open form.

30. Compound words • 87

Following is a brief summary of kinds of compounds and the forms in which they should appear.

NOUN COMPOUNDS DERIVED FROM A VERB AND ENDING IN -ER OR -ING

Many such compounds are hyphenated:

baby-sitter   face-lifting
well-digger   apple-polishing

Still, this type contains more forms written solid or open than hyphenated:

troublemaker   lawn mower
proofreader   freight handler
housekeeper   horse trader

The hyphen is most useful when it helps avoid confusion in meaning. For example, a well digger might be a digger who feels well, but a well-digger is a digger of wells. Such compounds are derived from a verb and its object:

He digs wells. He is a well-digger.

COMPOUNDS DERIVED FROM A VERB AND ADVERB

Modern English uses countless verb-adverb combinations:

take over   make up
drive in   hand out

These are never hyphenated when used as verbs:

Russia planned to take over the government of Lithuania.
You can drive in to the bank window.
He let us make up the exam.
You may hand out the tickets.

When used as compound nouns or adjectives, however, they are usually hyphenated:

88 • Arbitrary Marks and Usages

> Russia engineered a take-over of the government of Lithuania.
> The bank's drive-in window is open at nine-thirty.
> He gave us a make-up exam.
> Don't give us a hand-out.

A few such compounds in common usage are written solid. For example:

> blowup   comeback

But they are never written in open form when used as compound nouns or adjectives.

COMPOUND ADJECTIVES DERIVED FROM PARTICIPLES

These are usually hyphenated, and are almost invariably hyphenated when used before the noun:

> hot-tempered   sweet-smelling
> wide-eyed   fast-moving
> double-spaced   long-suffering
> smoke-filled   wide-ranging

This group includes the large number of compounds with *well* as the first element:

> well-advised   well-groomed
> well-known   well-meaning

Such compounds with an adverbial preposition as the first element are usually written solid:

> upswept   incoming
> outspoken   ongoing

COMPOUND ADJECTIVES IN WHICH THE TWO ELEMENTS RETAIN INDEPENDENT MEANING

This type of compound is always hyphenated:

> black-white confrontation
> husband-wife team

30. Compound words • 89

    purple-gold sunset
    cotton-nylon fabric

COMPOUND VERBS DERIVED FROM A VERB AND A PHRASE, OR VERB AND ADVERB

Such compounds are hyphenated:

    water-ski   double-space
    power-dive   heat-treat

Similar verbs are often derived from compound nouns, in which case they may be solid as well as hyphenated:

    sandbag   watermark   snowshoe

PHRASES USED AS COMPOUND NOUNS OR ADJECTIVES

A phrase should *never*, in fact, be hyphenated unless it is used as a single compound word.

    NORMAL PHRASE:
        He is a man of many talents.
        I gave him a surprise in a box.
    PHRASE USED AS COMPOUND:
        He is a jack-of-all-trades.
        I gave him a jack-in-the-box.

Phrases are always hyphenated when taken out of normal position and placed in front of a noun as a compound adjective:

    The error was corrected on the spot.
    They made an on-the-spot correction.

    He drove down the middle of the road.
    He followed a middle-of-the-road philosophy.

    OTHERS:
        a no-nonsense position
        a down-in-the-mouth expression
        an off-the-face hat

a devil-may-care attitude
an out-of-date coat
an unheard-of proposition

In informal writing, such hyphenated compounds are occasionally carried to great lengths:

She gave me a who-do-you-think-you-are look.
I received a don't-call-me-I'll-call-you reply.
Here is an off-the-top-of-my-head comment.

But be careful *not* to hyphenate phrases when they are used as part of normal sentence structure:

Who do you think you are?
Don't call me, I'll call you.
She wore her hat off the face.
The devil may care, but I don't.
Her coat is out of date.
The proposition is unheard of.
Here is a comment off the top of my head.

That is, word combinations are usually not hyphenated in a normal predicate position. They are hyphenated only when used attributively — that is, as a modifier placed before another word rather than after.

SUSPENDED COMPOUNDS

Hyphenate each part of a suspended compound:

a 10- or 12-foot pole
a meat- or vegetable-eating animal

HYPHENATION FOR CLARIFICATION

A hyphen may be used to connect two words as a compound in order to avoid confusion of meaning, when ordinarily they would be written in open form:

small-business representatives
slow-moving van

Most noun-plus-noun and adjective-plus-noun compounds are written in either open or solid form, more rarely with the hyphen:

raisin bread
word group
white elephant
cookbook
bluebird
freeway

However, when used before nouns as modifiers, the open forms are frequently hyphenated:

raisin-bread sandwich
word-group modifiers
white-elephant sale

Compound nouns whose first element would normally take an apostrophe omit the apostrophe when written in solid form:

menswear   foolscap   cockscomb

31. THE HYPHEN SOMETIMES SEPARATES THE PREFIX FROM A BASE WORD

HYPHENATE WHEN THE BASE WORD BEGINS WITH A CAPITAL LETTER

pro-British
pre-Columbian
anti-Stalinist

HYPHENATE WHEN TWO LIKE VOWELS COME TOGETHER

semi-invalid
anti-imperialism
de-emphasize

However, common usage leads in some cases to widespread occurrence of the solid style:

cooperate
preeminent

HYPHENATE MOST WORDS WITH THE PREFIXES SELF- AND EX-

self-employed
ex-president

HYPHENATE THE PREFIX RE- WHENEVER NECESSARY TO DISTINGUISH FROM WORDS OTHERWISE SPELLED IDENTICALLY

re-cover, recover
re-creation, recreation
re-dress, redress

A hyphenated prefix is sometimes used with a compound:

ex-vice president

In such cases, it may be wise to hyphenate all parts of the compound, in order to avoid the appearance that the prefix attaches only to the first word of it:

ex-Democratic minority leader
ex-Democratic-minority-leader

That is, he is an ex-leader, not an ex-Democrat. The hyphens are awkward, but they are the only way to indicate the right meaning.

32. HYPHENATE NUMBERS FROM TWENTY-ONE THROUGH NINETY-NINE

EXAMPLES: thirty-five
thirty-fifth

Numbers above one hundred are frequently written in numerical form rather than spelled out. However, if they

32. Hyphenating numbers • 93

are spelled out, the hyphen is used only in the forms "twenty-one" through "ninety-nine":

one hundred twenty-two
forty-three thousand
one thousand six hundred and sixty-seventh

Apply the same rule to fractions:

seven sixteenths
one sixty-fourth
twenty-three sixty-fourths

Fractions involving numbers of one hundred or greater are best written in numerical form.

33. THE APOSTROPHE WITH S SHOWS THE POSSESSIVE CASE

The apostrophe is largely meaningless. In only a few instances, as you will see below, does it serve to differentiate one possible meaning from another. In the context of a sentence, a possessive noun is almost invariably distinguishable from a plural, just as it is in speech, where we do not have apostrophes or other special signals to show the difference. The relation of words in the sentence makes it sufficiently clear.

But in spite of occasional campaigns to get rid of the apostrophe, it is too well established to ignore. When in doubt, refer to the following summary of current practice.

SINGULAR NOUNS THAT END IN A SOUND OTHER THAN S OR Z ADD AN APOSTROPHE AND S TO FORM THE POSSESSIVE CASE

girl's dress
dog's leg
senate's policy

94 • Arbitrary Marks and Usages

If a noun ends in a silent *s*, add an apostrophe and *s* anyway, since the rule is governed by the last *spoken* sound:

the corps's spirit
Descartes's philosophy

PLURAL NOUNS ENDING IN A SOUND OTHER THAN S OR Z ADD AN APOSTROPHE AND S TO FORM THE POSSESSIVE CASE

men's room
women's magazines
children's clothing

SINGULAR NOUNS ENDING IN AN S OR Z SOUND MAY ADD AN APOSTROPHE AND S TO FORM THE POSSESSIVE CASE

Be guided by pronunciation. Most single-syllable words and words accented on the last syllable add both the apostrophe and *s*:

Keats's
the class's grade average
James's sister
remorse's overpowering influence

However, words of more than one syllable *not* accented on the last syllable (and ending in an *s* or *z* sound) may add the apostrophe alone, without the extra *s*:

Socrates' philosophy
Dickens' novels
for righteousness' sake

Usage in such cases is divided. The possessive *s* seems generally to be omitted whenever it would be awkward or difficult

33. Apostrophe and possessive case • 95

to pronounce. Usage, then, may vary from one context to another or from one writer to another:

> President Adams's wife, President Adams' servants
> the seamstress's work, the seamstress' Sunday afternoon
> Congress' privilege, Congress's privilege

MOST PLURAL NOUNS ENDING IN AN S OR Z SOUND ADD THE APOSTROPHE ALONE TO SHOW THE POSSESSIVE CASE

These almost invariably add only the apostrophe, without the extra *s*:

> students' demands
> dentists' organization
> the gods' will

A few words form plurals by internal change rather than by adding *s* (man-men, mouse-mice). When such plurals end in an *s* sound, the possessive is formed by adding both apostrophe and *s*:

> the geese's flight
> the mice's nest

POSSESSIVE FORMS OF PRONOUNS

Indefinite pronouns take the apostrophe and *s*:

> someone's
> anybody's
> everyone's

Possessive pronouns never take an apostrophe:

> his   ours
> hers   yours
> its   theirs

34. THE APOSTROPHE WITH S IS USED TO SHOW THE PLURAL OF LETTERS AND NUMERALS ONLY

Possessive and plural forms should not be confused. Notice that an apostrophe plus *s* is *added to* a plural form which already ends in *s*:

students, students' demands
geese, geese's flight
the Johnsons, the Johnsons' house

That is, the apostrophe only shows that the plural is also possessive. It does not change a singular to a plural.

Some confused writers do not distinguish between a possessive and a simple plural, but use an apostrophe plus *s* where a simple *s* is in order.

WRONG: I bought three book's.

You may have seen illiterate roadside signs, like the following:

EGG'S
THE JOHNSON'S [Is there only one Johnson?]

However, an apostrophe plus *s* does properly show a plural in a few special instances where plurals are formed with symbols rather than with words:

The 8's and 10's are too large.
There was a severe depression in the late 1830's.
She already knows her ABC's.
The word *preference* has three *e*'s.

Some authorities recommend omitting such apostrophes when no confusion results:

ABCs
1830s
8s and 10s

34. Apostrophe and plurals • 97

But the apostrophe is useful when it serves to prevent misreading:

The *a*'s and *i*'s in your handwriting resemble *o*'s and *e*'s.
The *a*s and *i*s in your handwriting resemble *o*s and *e*s.

Of course, small numerals can be written out as words, in which case they are treated like any other plurals:

The eights and tens are too large.

35. THE APOSTROPHE STANDS FOR THE OMISSION OF LETTERS OR NUMERALS

Words which are telescoped by the omission of letters are called contractions. Notice how they differ from abbreviations: an abbreviation is a condensed form for spelling purposes only; it is always pronounced as if it were written out in full, whereas a contraction is pronounced as it is spelled.

CONTRACTION: didn't (did not)
ABBREVIATION: Vt. (Vermont)

In the contraction, an apostrophe is placed in the position where one or more letters have been omitted:

don't (do not)
she'll (she will)
he'll've (he will have)
rock'n'roll (rock and roll)

Dialect writers are fond of portraying contractions in what is supposed to be actual speech:

Ol' rockin' chair's got me.

However, a little of this kind of stylizing goes a long way, and most readers are wearied by the thought of pages of dialogue like the following (from G. W. Cable's novel *The Grandissimes*):

98 • Arbitrary Marks and Usages

"Dat me w'at pass in Rue Royale ev'y mawnin' holl'in' 'Bé calas touts chauds,' and singin'; don't you know?"

In informal writing, years are frequently contracted in similar fashion, as they might be pronounced:

the class of '62
the crash of '29
the blizzard of '87
the gold rush of '49

36. ABBREVIATIONS

An abbreviation may take two forms: a shortened form of a word (apt. for apartment), or a set of capitalized initial letters (U.S.A. for United States of America, T. S. Eliot for Thomas Stearns Eliot).

With regard to punctuation, the only problem is whether to use a period following the abbreviation or the individual letters. (For spelling, you must refer to handbooks on style, dictionaries of abbreviations, or a section on abbreviations which you are likely to find at the back of your dictionary. *Webster's Seventh New Collegiate Dictionary,* for example, lists some 1800 abbreviations in an appendix. A reference librarian can guide you to specialized works.)

American usage requires a period after titles: Mr. Johnson, Pres. Nixon, Mrs. Lawford, Dr. Andrews, Capt. Kurtz, Sen. Scott.

And after the initials of a proper name: T. S. Eliot, J. F. Kennedy, James T. Farrell.

Usage is divided on placing a period after each letter in the abbreviated names of organizations or bureaus. You are more likely to use periods when the letters are pronounced individually (A.I.A., W.C.T.U., D.A.R.). Periods are usually omitted when the letters form an acronym—that is, a new word formed by pronouncing the letters as if they spelled a word (CARE, UNICEF, NATO, UFO, WAVE).

Current practice seems inclined toward simplifying punctuation, thus favoring the omission of periods. Long-established abbreviations with an air of conservatism, like the M.A., M.D., and Ph.D. degrees, are likely to continue preserving the more conservative use of the period, while new ones, like LSD, tend to appear almost from the beginning without them. Others, like m.p.h. (miles per hour) may appear in several forms: m.p.h., M.P.H., mph, MPH. Editors, writers, and teachers simply exercise their personal preferences, based on what they feel is most widely accepted current practice or on preferences codified in a style book.

Shortened words, or telescoped spellings, on the other hand, are almost invariably followed by a period:

dept.   exch.
geol.   constr.
Wed.   bldg.

37. ARBITRARY USES OF COMMAS

LETTERS

The salutation of an informal letter is followed by a comma:

Dear Alex,

A formal salutation (business letter) is followed by a colon:

Dear Sir:

The complimentary close is followed by a comma in all letters:

Yours truly,
Sincerely,
With love,

NAMES

A comma separates a name from a degree or honorary title that follows:

Milton R. Standish, M.D.
Gregory Baker, M.A., Ph.D., Litt. D.

Such titles are treated grammatically as appositives. In sentence context, place a second comma after the title:

Marguerite Wilson, M.S., F.A.C.P., Vice President, will be guest speaker.

A comma separates first and last names when they are reversed. Titles are placed at the end.

Greenfield, William B.
Arbuckle, Harvey Francis, Jr.
Wilson, Marguerite, M.D.
Hatfield, Conrad, Lt.Gen.

ADDRESSES AND PLACE NAMES

Commas separate street, city, state, and country (no comma between state and zip-code number):

1424 West Annandale Blvd., Springfield, Michigan 48511, U.S.A.

In sentence context, a comma follows the last item in a place name or address:

Salinas, California, was then only a sleepy little town.
They lived at 1424 West Annandale Blvd., Springfield, Michigan, for three years.

DATES

Two forms are currently in acceptable use. When the day of the month comes first, commas are often omitted throughout:

We arrived on 17 January 1963 for a brief visit.

When the day of the month comes second, commas are traditionally used after each number:

We arrived on January 17, 1963, for a brief visit.

A comma is important to separate the two numbers for ease in reading. However, the comma is now often omitted after the year:

We arrived on January 17, 1963 for a brief visit.

Usage is also equally divided when the day of the month is not given:

We arrived in January, 1963, for a brief visit.
We arrived in January, 1963 for a brief visit.
We arrived in January 1963 for a brief visit.

To summarize, the only place where a comma is unavoidable in a date is between two numbers that fall together:

April 3, 1971

All other commas may be safely omitted, although it is only fair to point out that students are frequently taught to follow the more conservative practice of using the maximum number of commas.

NUMBERS

Numbers of four or more digits are divided by commas into groups of three to indicate hundreds, thousands, millions, and so on.

1,302
341,302
7,341,302

However, commas are ordinarily omitted from such numbers when they are used in specialized ways: telephone numbers, street addresses, postal zip-codes, page numbers, social security and other serial numbers, fractions, and large decimals. The advent of the computing machine, the credit card, and direct long-distance telephone dialing has familiarized nearly everyone with lengthy code numbers divided into groups of numerals no longer separated by commas.

38. SLANT, OR VIRGULE

A slanted line (/) is familiar in informal and hasty writing as a handy way to abbreviate dates and indicate the abbreviation "in care of":

3/16/71
c/o

It is commonly used to indicate alternatives:

You may send cash and/or stamps.

The writer must be warned, however, that the above uses are considered out of place in formal writing, and are appropriate only to practical business situations or informal letter writing.

The slant has one acceptable formal use, and that is to indicate the division between lines of poetry when they are run together as prose:

"The mind is its own place," Milton's Satan says, "and in itself/Can make a Heaven of Hell, a Hell of Heaven."

39. ARBITRARY USES OF THE COLON

The colon performs certain mechanical functions of dividing elements while holding them together in set relationships.

SALUTATIONS IN BUSINESS LETTERS
(SEE ALSO SECTION 37 ABOVE)

Dear Sir:

SUBTITLES

Although a colon does not always appear on the title page of a book between a title and subtitle, it should be so placed when citing such titles in full:

The Mirror and the Lamp: Romantic Theory and the Critical Tradition

TIME TELLING

Hours, minutes, and seconds are separated by colons:

1:25
3:47:52

40. CAPITALIZATION

There is perhaps some question as to whether capitalization belongs in a treatment of punctuation, since it seems more properly an aspect of spelling. Nevertheless, it is given here for convenient reference.

Capitalizing has become increasingly simplified through the years. While once it was employed to emphasize almost any important word, it has now settled down into a set of fairly standard conventions. Generally speaking, all capitals fall under one of the following headings:

1. Proper names
2. First words in sentences, quotations, and lines of poetry
3. First and main words in titles

PROPER NAMES

A proper name is the name of a specific individual entity, as opposed to a general class of things: Mexico as opposed to "nation," John Smith as opposed to "man," Chevrolet as opposed to "automobile," Rover as opposed to "dog," World War I as opposed to "war," Tuesday as opposed to "day."

104 • Arbitrary Marks and Usages

Simple as this distinction is in principle, it can be complicated in application. The following guidelines will help eliminate confusion.

A. The names of persons and pet animals (including nicknames) are always capitalized without exception:

Joseph   Spotty
Joe   Baby

B. The names of nations, peoples, races, tribes, and languages are capitalized without exception:

France   Navajo
Arab   English
Negro   African

C. Most other words derived from both of the above categories are also capitalized:

Elizabethan   French   Afro-American
Victorian   Latinate   Indo-European
Stalinist   Siamese   Indian

However, a derivative from a proper name occasionally loses its capital, especially when the connection with its source becomes faint through common usage. For example, the words lynch, macadamize, sadism, masochism, pasteurize, and spoonerism are seldom associated with the names of Charles Lynch, John L. McAdam, the Marquis de Sade, Leopold von Sacher-Masoch, Louis Pasteur, and William A. Spooner, which are their sources. Even so, usage may vary with no apparent rhyme or reason. We capitalize French door, French horn, and French dressing, but not french fries; Swiss steak, but not dotted swiss; Anglo, but not anglicize. Generally, *verbs* derived from proper names are not capitalized: frenchify, germanize, japanize, americanize, latinize. Adjectives and nouns are more usually capitalized: Germanic, Freudian, Spanish, Englishman.

Even though these guidelines are true for most cases, there are many exceptions. The only safe course when in doubt is to consult a dictionary.

D. Honorary, academic, professional, military, and business titles are capitalized when used before proper names:

>   Queen Elizabeth I
>   Professor Northrop Frye
>   Dr. Benjamin Spock
>   Senator Jacob Javits
>   General Louis B. Hershey
>   Saint Thomas Aquinas
>   President Richard M. Nixon
>   Archbishop Fulton J. Sheen
>   Supreme Court Justice Hugo Black

(Note that this rule does not extend to ordinary names of occupations: commentator Walter Cronkite, playwright George Bernard Shaw.) Titles are not capitalized when they *follow* the proper name. In that position, they are treated as common nouns:

>   Elizabeth I, queen of England
>   Richard M. Nixon, president of the United States
>   Benjamin Spock, doctor of pediatrics
>   Jacob Javits, senator from New York
>   Hugo Black, justice of the Supreme Court

Similarly, such titles are never capitalized when they are used in a generic sense—that is, when they refer to the position but not to an individual:

>   five generals
>   a senator
>   a president
>   two prime ministers
>   a Supreme Court justice
>   a king
>   a secretary of state
>   an archbishop
>   three saints

When a specific individual is referred to by his title alone, usage is divided. It is sometimes capitalized, sometimes not:

The President will hold a news conference on Monday night.
The president will tour five Western states.

Writers wishing to express respect for the position will probably be more inclined to capitalize.

Nicknames used as parts of titles are capitalized:

Ivan the Terrible
Peter the Great
Pepin the Short

Titles used in direct address are capitalized, even though the name may not be used:

Your Highness
Your Eminence
Your Majesty
Mr. President

E. Epithets used in place of proper names are capitalized:

Old Hickory
Old Nick
the Iron Duke

F. Names of official governmental bodies and documents are capitalized:

the Federal Reserve Bank
the Supreme Court
the Declaration of Independence
the Bill of Rights
the Interstate Commerce Commission
Tennessee Valley Authority
the Constitution

However, general references are usually not capitalized:

an interpretation of the constitution
a court decision
various federal agencies and commissions

40. Capitalization • 107

Similarly, names of political parties and other organizations are capitalized, but general references are not:

    the Democratic party (but: democratic ideals)
    American Federation of Labor (but: labor unions)
    the University of California (but: he attends the university)

Political terms are capitalized when they form part of a proper name, but not otherwise:

        Republic of Liberia
        State of Illinois
        Province of Quebec
        Commonwealth of Massachusetts
        New York City
BUT: Liberia is a republic
        five small states, three provinces, an empire, the city of New York

Following the same rule that applies to individual persons, a reference to a specific political entity may or may not be capitalized when used alone:

    He works for the State of Illinois.
    He works for the State (or state).

  G. Geographical terms are capitalized when they form part of a proper name, but are not capitalized when used in a general sense:

San Francisco Bay	Rock of Gibraltar
Clear Lake	Great Plains
Missouri River	North Miami Beach
Gulf Stream	Florida Keys
Isle of Man	Bering Strait
Grand Banks	Ivory Coast
Cape Cod	Japan Trough
Great Lakes	Firth of Forth
BUT: Missouri River valley	Atlantic coast
Pacific beaches	the plains of central Russia
Canadian mountains	Sargasso sea

Points of the compass are capitalized only when they refer to regions:

the South	the Southwest	Southern hospitality
the West	the Northwest	Western cowboys
the East	the Midwest	Northern industry
the North	North America	Midwestern agriculture

BUT: drive east
head west
a wind from the north
south of Ohio

Similarly, geographical divisions of the world are usually capitalized:

Orient
Middle East
New World

H. Names and adjectives referring to the Deity are usually capitalized, and sometimes pronouns as well:

God	Yahweh
His Son	Holy Spirit
Allah	Almighty
Lord	Providence

Conservative usage sometimes capitalizes Who, Thou, His, and the like, even when the context makes the reference clear.

I. Personifications are often capitalized to distinguish them from a word used in a general sense:

Nature	Truth
Honor	Freedom
Spring	Night
Death	Sorrow

It must be noted, however, that such personifications are currently out of fashion, and seldom used by good writers, except facetiously.

J. Names beginning with *De* are usually capitalized when American, but are usually not capitalized when foreign:

De Kruif	de Gaulle
De Mille	de la Mare
De Voto	de Soto
	de Valera

Similarly, other particles appearing in foreign names are usually not capitalized:

Leonardo da Vinci
Ludwig van Beethoven

But unless you are familiar with the name, it is best to consult a dictionary, encyclopedia, or some other authority. Exceptions do occur.

Generally speaking, words should not be capitalized simply to imply importance unless they are usually so capitalized.

FIRST WORDS IN SENTENCES, QUOTATIONS, AND LINES OF POETRY

The best-known rule of capitalization is that first words in sentences are always capitalized. Any sentence in this book will illustrate it.

The first word of a quotation, or a line of dialogue, is capitalized:

Jeremy asked, "Is it time?"
According to Emerson, "A foolish consistency is the hobgoblin of little minds."

Similarly, the first word of a question incorporated in a sentence may be capitalized even though it is not actually a quotation:

I ask, Can we afford the moral cost?

Remember, however, that fragmented quotations are not capitalized when incorporated in a sentence:

Fashion critics called the queen's style of dress "dowdy" and "matronly."

First lines of poetry are traditionally capitalized:

Five years have past; five summers, with the length
Of five long winters! and again I hear
These waters...

However, much contemporary poetry no longer follows this convention. When quoting, follow the precise pattern of the original:

What is our innocence,
what is our guilt? All are
naked, none is safe.

FIRST AND MAIN WORDS IN TITLES

The best approach to capitalization in titles of books, articles, plays, periodicals, and the like, is to remember the few kinds of words which are *not* capitalized:

articles (*a, an,* and *the*)
prepositions (*of, to, with, at,* and the like)
conjunctions (*and, but, or,* and the like)

All these are capitalized, however, if they are first or last words in a title:

"A Hope to Build On"
On Getting a Living
Crime and Punishment
The Road to Damascus
A Tale of a Tub
Journal of the American Medical Association

The length of a word is not the sole reason for capitalization, since pronouns (like *he, it, she*) are always capitalized. Some authorities, however, recommend capitalizing the longer prepositions and conjunctions, such as *between, whenever, before.*

Be careful to distinguish a preposition from an adverb. An adverb in a title is always capitalized, though a preposition is not:

Running Away from Myself

The article *the* is usually not capitalized when it is used in conjunction with titles of newspapers and magazines:

the *Ladies Home Journal*
the *San Francisco Chronicle*

The word *magazine* is also usually not capitalized:

Time magazine

However, if the words "the" or "magazine" constitute an accepted part of a title, and are usually included when referring to it, they should also be capitalized and italicized:

The New York Times
McCall's Magazine

FIRST-PERSON PRONOUN

The pronoun *I* is always capitalized in English.

41. ITALICIZATION

Italics, like capitalization, are not strictly a matter of punctuation, but are included here for convenience.
Italics are indicated in manuscript by underlining.

ITALICIZING FOR EMPHASIS

Numerous examples may be found in the works of Edgar Allan Poe, who was fond of italicizing words, phrases, and even entire sentences for emphasis:

Not thus he appeared — assuredly not *thus* — in the vivacity of his waking hours.

Was it, in truth, within the bounds of human possibility, that *what I now saw* was the result, merely, of the habitual practice of this sarcastic imitation?

Italics so used imply greater stress when read aloud. Excitable writers are urged to use such emphasis sparingly.

TITLES OF BOOKS, PLAYS, MOTION PICTURES, LONG POEMS, WORKS OF ART, AND PERIODICALS

The general rule is that shorter poems, chapters or parts of books and titles of short stories are *not* italicized but enclosed in quotation marks:

"A Good Man is Hard to Find"
"The Idiot Boy"
Chapter I: "The Prison-Door," of *The Scarlet Letter*

But italicize book-length or long, complete works, and titles of works of art:

Dostoevsky's *Crime and Punishment*
Leonardo's *Mona Lisa*
Milton's *Paradise Lost*
Tennessee Williams' *The Glass Menagerie*
Boston Globe
Harvard Law Review
Midnight Cowboy

FOREIGN WORDS AND PHRASES

In the context of English sentences, foreign words and phrases are usually italicized if they have not yet become familiar or widespread in English usage, or if they may be unfamiliar to the particular reading audience. No rule can be laid down, since practice varies widely.

The governments are seeking a *rapprochement* on the immigrant labor problem.
Ankle-length coats are de rigeur this season.

41. Italicization • 113

WORDS REFERRED TO AS WORDS

EXAMPLE: The word *and* is sometimes omitted from a series of three or more items.

While italicizing is usually preferred, such words may also be enclosed in quotation marks:

The word "and" is sometimes omitted from a series of three or more items.

The same practice is extended to references to entire phrases or to individual letters of the alphabet:

The letter *e* is the most frequently used letter in English.
The phrase *don't pay him no mind* is common only in the South.

When such a word or letter occurs in a sentence or heading that is already italicized, making further italicizing impossible, it reverts to a standard typeface:

Plural nouns ending in an s *or* z *sound*

MINOR USES OF ITALICS

Names of ships, aircraft, and trains have traditionally been italicized. However, with the decline in train travel, famous individual runs once known by popular names no longer exist. With the growth of air travel, passengers ordinarily identify their airplane simply by a flight number. Ships, however, still retain an identity. And any reference to aircraft, trains, or ships, historically or contemporaneously, may still be italicized:

China Clipper
the *Skylark*
the *Queen Elizabeth II*
the *Titanic*

PART III
Punctuating Imaginative Writing

Occasionally a student discovers that novelists and poets often do not abide by the "rules" of punctuation. Naturally, he wonders why he cannot do the same. Usually he is told that he must first master the rules before earning the right to break them. This answer places the issue on an authoritarian basis which seldom appeals. There is actually a much better reason for mastering the "rules." A study of imaginative uses of punctuation will show that departures from conventional usage are careful and deliberate, and often make no sense unless one takes standard punctuation as a reference point.

The poet e. e. cummings, for example, in eliminating capital letters from his own name and from the pronoun I, implies that he is turning these words into common rather than proper nouns. It suggests not only humility, but universality rather than individuality. These implications are meaningful only because the reader is familiar with the customary reasons for capitalizing. Forgoing these capital letters is not simply a rule-breaking gimmick, but a reasonable and imaginative variation on traditional conventions. The poet knew perfectly well why certain words are usually capitalized, and he did not change the rules simply to cloak his ignorance. He enlarged the meaning of his poems thereby.

With this principle in mind, we will first look at the standard forms of punctuation in imaginative writing, and then show examples of purposeful variations.

42. PUNCTUATING DIALOGUE

Every change to a different speaker should be indicated by a paragraph indention, no matter how short the lines of dialogue may be:

"I saw you out of the window," he said. "Didn't want to interrupt you. What were you doing? Burying your money?"
"You lazy bum!"
"Been working for the common good? Splendid. I want you to do that every morning."
"Come on," I said. "Get up."
"What? Get up? I never get up."
He climbed into bed and pulled the sheet up to his chin.
(Ernest Hemingway, *The Sun Also Rises*)

Attributions ("he said," "she said") may come before or after the speech, or at a break in the middle of it. Punctuation follows the example above, the same pattern described in Section 26, "How to quote from another author's work."

Dialogue and narration are often blended together in a single paragraph, as long as the spoken words are those of a single character:

"Dilsey," Mother says on the stairs. Quentin ran up the stairs, passing her. "Quentin," Mother says, "You, Quentin." Quentin ran on. I could hear her when she reached the top, then in the hall. Then the door slammed.   (William Faulkner, *The Sound and the Fury*)

Readers are so accustomed to the long-standing convention of indicating each change of speaker with a fresh paragraph indention that failure to do so will create puzzlement and annoyance. The reader must not lose track of who is speaking. Innovators and experimental stylists seldom depart from this practice, and, in fact, take pains to make clear the shifts among speakers.

42. Punctuating dialogue • 117

Dialogue must sound like natural spoken language, at least if the writer operates within modern standards of realism. For this reason, sentences may freely be grammatically "incorrect" by the standards that govern formal prose. Punctuation can be adjusted to the pauses and intonations of the speaking voice:

"D'you know it, Del, you kinda remind me o' my sister Janey honest you do. Dodgast it, she's amounting to something all right.... She's awful pretty too..." (John Dos Passos, *1919*)

Here, commas are omitted (after "Janey" and "pretty") to indicate the lack of pause, the running together of phrases. The points of ellipsis indicate a thoughtful pause, a moment of silence.

In *The Sound and the Fury*, Faulkner narrates each section of the story from a different point of view. In the first section, the action is seen through the eyes of the mentally retarded Benjy. This is how Benjy hears dialogue:

"Let me have two bits." Luster said.
"What for." Jason said.
"To go to the show tonight." Luster said.
"I thought Dilsey was going to get a quarter from Frony for you." Jason said.

Each speech ends with a period rather than the expected comma or question mark. This technique projects the blankness of Benjy's understanding, which hears words but cannot follow the drift of meaning. Benjy's mental world lacks punctuation marks that show the subtlety of thought.

43. NARRATION BY A FICTIONAL CHARACTER

After *Huckleberry Finn*, a great many modern writers have narrated novels or short stories through the mouth of a selected fictional character who participates in the action and writes as an eye-witness. Generally, such fictional voices suggest a

118 • Imaginative Writing

high degree of intelligence and perceptiveness rather like the author's own. Nick Carroway, the narrator of Fitzgerald's *The Great Gatsby*, and Jake Barnes, of Hemingway's *The Sun Also Rises*, are educated, literate persons whose prose does not call for unusual or imaginative punctuation. They seem to be *writing* the story rather than *telling* it orally. Hemingway's manner is casual and conversational, but far removed from any dialectal peculiarities. Occasional sentences like the following combine an air of oral informality with standard narration:

> The lady who had him, her name was Frances, found toward the end of the second year that her looks were going, and her attitude toward Robert changed from one of careless possession and exploitation to the absolute determination that he should marry her.

Dialogue in such narratives is handled exactly as it is in fiction written from an objective (or author's) point of view. Punctuation is no different from that of standard prose.

Similarly, a narrative presented in the form of a diary or other written record, such as Nabokov's *Lolita*, generally follows standard punctuation throughout.

44. NARRATION FROM THE POINT OF VIEW OF A CHARACTER'S THOUGHTS

This perspective differs from that taken when a fictional character narrates in that it expresses what goes on inside his head, rather than what he writes down or tells aloud. It is a way of telling a story through the medium of a character's consciousness. Events and physical surroundings are presented as the character sees them and reacts to them:

> The band had been having a rest. Now they started again. And what they played was warm, sunny, yet there was a faint chill — a something, what was it? — not sadness, no, not sadness — a something that made you want to sing.   (Katherine Mansfield, "Miss Brill")

Notice that such narration is not presented in quotation marks, nor does it pretend to be the stream of words actually going on in the character's mind. It is written in the third person, blending the kind of vocabulary the character would use, and even the rhythm of her thoughts, in a narrative that tells the story of an inner experience. The punctuation follows all the regular standards set forth in Part I of this book, but requires a great deal of informal flexibility to match the casual flow of inner thoughts and reactions.

This method is widely used in modern fiction, and can be found in almost any novel or short story written since the 1920's.

It was a lousy trip. Joe was worried all the time about Del and about not making good and the deckcrew was a bunch of soreheads. The engines kept breaking down. *The Higginbotham* was built like a cheesebox and so slow there were days when they didn't make more'n thirty or forty miles against moderate headwinds.

(Dos Passos, *1919*)

It was useless. He couldn't read. He couldn't do anything. The wailing of the child pierced the drum of his ear. It was useless, useless! He was a prisoner for life. His arms trembled with anger and suddenly bending to the child's face he shouted:
"Stop!" (James Joyce, "A Little Cloud")

Dialogue in such narration is placed within quotation marks and is handled exactly like dialogue in any standard form of narrative. Notice that writers using this technique tend to omit commas more freely, to catch the effect of rapid conversation.

45. DIRECT QUOTATION OF A CHARACTER'S THOUGHTS

The increasing influence of psychology in fiction has caused writers to focus on the actual stream of words that pass through a character's consciousness. In a sense, this technique is another form of direct quotation, except that it quotes unspoken words rather than oral dialogue.

It would be possible to place such inner language within quotation marks and treat it the same as ordinary dialogue:

"Why am I here?" he wondered.

But fiction writers have attempted to expose the inner workings of a character's mind much more dramatically and directly than that. As a result, they have sought new techniques to give a greater sense of immediacy. The contents of the mind are often jumbled and fragmentary, and do not consist of orderly sentences.

John Dos Passos, in his trilogy of novels, *U.S.A.*, inserted brief sections entitled "The Camera Eye," which represent such fragments of the author's own consciousness:

> when the telegram came that she was dying (the streetcar wheels screeched round the bellglass like all the pencils on all the slates in all the schools) walking around Fresh Pond the smell of puddlewater willowbuds in the raw wind shrieking streetcar wheels rattling on loose trucks through the Boston suburbs grief isn't a uniform and go shock the Booch and drink wine for supper at the Lennox before catching the Federal

James Joyce wrote the entire last chapter of *Ulysses*, of over forty pages, in this manner, without punctuation or paragraph breaks. The chapter represents the interior monologue of Molly Bloom as she lies in bed at night. Here is a brief sample:

> telling me all her ailments she had too much old chat in her about politics and earthquakes and the end of the world let us have a bit of fun first God help the world if all the women were her sort down on bathingsuits and lownecks of course nobody wanted her to wear I suppose she was pious because no man would look at her twice

Such extremely close attention to the character's private thoughts, without benefit of logical sentence structure or punctuation, is often hard going for the reader. More frequently a writer will simply blend such "stream of consciousness" into a more conventional narrative. The reader moves into it and out again. Such mixed forms of narration, blending objectivity, inner point of view, and inner monologue, are actually much more common than pure and continuous quotation from a character's thoughts. Quotation marks are usually not used.

45. Quotation of thoughts

> Another slice of bread and butter: three, four: right. She didn't like her plate full. Right. He turned from the tray, lifted the kettle off the hob and set it sideways on the fire. It sat there, dull and squat, its spout stuck out. Cup of tea soon. Good. Mouth dry. The cat walked stiffly round a leg of the table with tail on high. (Joyce, *Ulysses*)

Despite the lack of quotation marks, the reader is easily able to distinguish between words quoted from the character's mind and the surrounding context of narration. Quotation marks are then reserved for spoken dialogue alone.

However, a problem arises when the character's stream of thoughts includes a quotation from someone else. Should quotation marks be used in such an instance? To do so might confuse the quoted material with dialogue and give the impression that it is being heard rather than remembered. But not to set it apart in some way would fail to show that it is someone else's words rather than the character's. This problem is usually solved by italicizing such material:

> He began to invent sentences and phrases from the notice which his book would get. "*Mr. Chandler has the gift of easy and graceful verse.*"..."*A wistful sadness pervades these poems.*"..."*The Celtic note.*" It was a pity his name was not more Irish-looking.
> (Joyce, "A Little Cloud")

Here Joyce used both quotation marks and italics. But it is the italics which indicate that the words are only in Chandler's reverie.

In *The Sound and the Fury*, William Faulkner used italics to differentiate the separate levels of time that occur simultaneously in the mind. When the present tense of the character's thoughts is interrupted by a memory, the words shift to italics:

> Shreve has a bottle in his trunk. *Aren't you even going to open it* Mr. and Mrs. Jason Richmond Compson announce the *Three times.* Days. *Aren't you even going to open it* marriage of their daughter Candace *that liquor teaches you to confuse the means with the end.*

Faulkner used italics even more extensively in *Absalom, Absalom!* to indicate the complex shifting back and forth in time which is a characteristic of the inner mental world, in one instance italicizing virtually all of a chapter, some thirty-eight pages.

46. CAPITALIZATION

Joyce, Faulkner, and Dos Passos, as we have seen in the examples above, freely omitted capital letters from what would normally be the first word of a sentence or fragment. They did this, however, only when they wished to run the sentences together in a way that suggests the unbroken flow of silent language in the mind. Otherwise, their capitalization follows ordinary conventions.

Capitals may be used for irony or to show the special importance of certain words to a character. It becomes a form of stress:

> "He's involved in a big deal."
> "What kind of Big Deal?"

47. QUOTING OTHER WORKS IN A FICTIONAL CONTEXT

Words of popular songs, poetry, newspaper articles or headlines, ritualistic prayers, and other linguistic materials from real life are occasionally quoted verbatim in the context of fiction. When they form part of a character's stream of thought or awareness, they are frequently italicized. For example, Stephen Dedalus, in Joyce's *Ulysses*, remembers the rite of extreme unction at his mother's death:

The ghost candle to light her agony. Ghostly light on the tortured face. Her hoarse loud breath rattling in horror, while all prayed on their knees. Her eyes on me to strike me down. *Liliata rutilantium te confessorum turma circumdet: iubilantium te virginum chorus excipiat.*

Ulysses is filled with scraps of poetry, songs, quotations from literature, advertising, and the like, which Joyce italicized consistently. His practice has been followed by many other writers. Such italicized material may be either worked into the context of a paragraph or printed separately so it stands apart.

48. COMPOUND WORDS

Another of Joyce's innovations, imitated by many other writers, is the coining of new compound words. Compounding is characteristic of modern English, and Joyce simply recognized and developed its artistic usefulness. His compounds are usually either nouns or adjectives, formed by blending two words into a fresh term that suggests a richer sense of concrete detail:

> woodshadows, wavewhite, muskperfumed, dewsilky, sweettoned, glowlamps

Even ordinary semicompounds, normally written as separate words or hyphenated, are printed as single words:

> coalsmoke, shavingbowl, waistcoatpocket, smokeplume, welloff

John Dos Passos also made a personal trademark out of such compounds:

> warcorrespondent, magazinewriter, ladyphotographer, novemberbrown, sleetlashed, worriedlooking, dirtstench, warmfeeling

Faulkner, too, and many minor writers, have found that compounding is a way to revitalize language. The only objection is that it can be easily overdone, and can develop into a mannerism that makes prose sound affected and artificial. But when sparingly and skillfully used, it is a valid extension of standard English usage.

49. PARAGRAPH LENGTH

Ordinary expository prose generally falls into structured paragraphs of two or three hundred words, each developing a point. The paragraph break therefore functions as a kind of punctuation: it shows the end of a larger unit of grouped sentences, just as the period shows the end of a single sentence.

In fiction, such breaks are determined by the nature of the narrative. A single word may be placed in a paragraph by itself for emphasis, like the word "Stop!" in Joyce's story "A Little Cloud," even though it forms a logical part of the preceding paragraph. At the opposite extreme, an entire chapter may be written continuously without any breaks at all. The writer can only be guided by his own purpose. Normally, however, a narrative will fall into paragraphs like expository prose, except when broken by dialogue.

Paragraph spacing is not usually considered a matter of punctuation, but rather of organization. Imaginative writers sometimes use spacing as an expressive device, either by running words together and eliminating an expected space, or by extending spaces between words. This practice is often expanded to include unconventional paragraph spacing as well.

50. SUMMARY OF PUNCTUATION IN FICTION

The older conventional form of narrative—up to approximately 1920—tended to be objective, and followed the same punctuation as any other prose writing. Part I of this book covers such punctuation. Many creative writers, of course, still write in this manner, and the standard principles are still valid.

However, the introduction of a new psychological dimension has brought the need for new ideas in punctuation. Distinctions must be made between spoken language and silent mental language, and even between the character's own mental words and remembered spoken words of others in his thoughts, and between different time levels in his thoughts. The new punctuation is still based on the old conventional practices, but has expanded them. The following principles are now widely accepted:

   1. Do not place quotation marks around either direct or indirect quotations from a character's thoughts. Use quotation marks only for actual spoken dialogue.
   2. Use italics for silent quotations within a character's thoughts, and also to distinguish other interruptive material within the stream of thoughts.
   3. Italics are optional for words of songs, passages from newspapers or other printed material.
   4. Punctuation may be omitted in order to give the impression of speed and continuous flow, whether in dialogue, thought, or narrative.
   5. Capitals at the beginning of sentences or fragments may also be omitted in order to give the impression of fragmentary thoughts or sensations.
   6. Paragraph breaks may be adapted to the length of material the writer wishes to keep all in one piece, whether it is as short as a single word or as long as a forty-page chapter.
   7. Compound words may be freely invented without the use of hyphens, in order to blend several impressions into one.

51. POETRY

   Traditional poetry in stanza form is composed of grammatically regular sentences fitted to a pattern of rhythms and rhymes. Punctuation, therefore, is exactly the same as it would be if the sentences were written as prose.
   The only difference: the first word in every line is capitalized.
   A punctuation mark is placed at the end of a line of poetry only when the sentence demands it, and not because it is the end of a line. If a sentence continues across the break between stanzas, no punctuation is required at the end of the stanza.
   If the poem contains quoted dialogue that continues through more than one stanza, quotation marks are placed at the beginning of each stanza just as they are at the beginning of a new

paragraph. No end-quotation marks are used, however, until the end of the quoted material is reached.

The following stanzas from Thomas Hardy's poem "The Man He Killed" illustrate all of these points:

> "I shot him dead because—
> Because he was my foe,
> Just so: my foe of course he was;
> That's clear enough; although
>
> "He thought he'd 'list, perhaps,
> Off-hand like—just as I—
> Was out of work—had sold his traps—
> No other reason why.
>
> "Yes; quaint and curious war is!
> You shoot a fellow down
> You'd treat if met where any bar is,
> Or help to half-a-crown."

The revolution in twentieth-century art, however, has modified these conventional practices in poetry as well as in prose. New ideas in punctuating poetry have closely paralleled those in fiction:

1. Omission of capital letters
2. Omission of commas and periods, and free use of spacing to indicate divisions, rather than punctuation marks
3. Freer use of more informal marks such as the dash and ellipsis

Marianne Moore, for example, has eliminated capital letters from the beginnings of lines, but uses them for first words of sentences. Note this example from "To a Snail":

> If "compression is the first grace of style,"
> you have it. Contractility is a virtue as
> modesty is a virtue.

Occasionally she uses the title as the opening words of the poem:

> The Wood-Weasel
> emerges daintily, the skunk—
> don't laugh—in sylvan black and white chipmunk
> regalia.

Most contemporary poems still consist of fairly regular sentences with standard punctuation, even though they may lack beginning-of-line capitals and may be irregularly spaced. Only when regular grammatical sentence form is broken down and the fragments are put back together for impressionistic effects (as Joyce, Dos Passos, and Faulkner did in prose) does special punctuation have to be adapted to it. An example from Hart Crane's "Powhatan's Daughter" demonstrates:

> Stick your patent name on a signboard
> brother—all over—going west—young man
> Tintex—Japalac—Certain-teed Overalls ads
> and lands sakes! under the new playbill ripped
> in the guaranteed corner—see Bert Williams what?

e. e. cummings introduced certain practices which are easily identifiable as typical of his work: omission of all capitals except for a few selected words, frequent use of parentheses, omission of commas and periods, running together of sentences in one line while splitting sentences or phrases across several lines, isolation of single words. The effect is often ironic or satirical, as in this example from "(ponder, darling, these busted statues)":

> (ponder, darling, these busted statues
> of yon motheaten forum be aware
> notice what hath remained
> —the stone cringes
> clinging to the stone, how obsolete
>
> lips utter their extant smile....
> remark
> a few deleted of texture
> or meaning monuments and dolls

> resist Them Greediest Paws of careful
> time all of which is extremely
> unimportant) whereas Life
>
> matters if or

The poem continues as an invitation to love-making, and it is evident that the lecture on Roman ruins, in stilted language, is placed within parentheses because it is irrelevant to the more "real" man-woman relationship that concerns the poet in the present. But the reader is forced to supply, mentally, the pauses and stops which would ordinarily be indicated by conventional punctuation:

> Ponder, darling, these busted statues.
> Of yon motheaten forum, be aware.
> Notice what hath remained—

All readers, of course, will not supply the same punctuation marks. The poet's ambiguity is presumably deliberate, and not the result of simply leaving out obvious marks which only need to be inserted.

Punctuation, then, in some modernist poetry is designed to disorient the reader from conventional attitudes and to underscore the poet's freshly individualized approach.

A century ago, Emily Dickinson wrote over 1500 poems, of which only three were published during her lifetime. Her punctuation was eccentrically individualistic—mostly dashes and numerous capital letters. When first published, it was "normalized" to meet current standards. But nowadays critics relish her unusual manuscript punctuation because it seems to be in the modern free spirit:

> Grand go the Years—in the Crescent—above them—
> Worlds scoop their Arcs—
> And Firmaments—row—
> Diadems—drop—and Doges—surrender—
> Soundless as dots—on a Disc of Snow—

But her precise reasons for these dashes remain a matter of mystery and speculation.

ALPHABETICAL REFERENCE GUIDE TO PUNCTUATION MARKS

Punctuation marks are listed below in alphabetical order, with brief explanations and examples. Each entry also refers you to the appropriate foregoing chapters where usage is explained and illustrated at greater length. Use this section as a manual for handy, quick reference.

<u>ABBREVIATIONS</u> SECTION 36

Use a period after every abbreviation which takes the form of a shortened word:

Mr., Gen., apt., etc., constr., int.

Usage is divided on placing a period after individual capital letters. If they are pronounced as a word, omit periods:

NASA, NATO, UNICEF, WAVE

If they are quite recent in origin, and in wide popular usage, omit periods:

LSD, TV, UFO

If they are long-standing, traditional, and conservative, use periods:

B.A., M.D., D.A.R.

Names of government bureaus and agencies, and other organizations frequently in the news, usually omit periods:

NAACP, ACLU, TVA

You are likely to see many such abbreviations written both ways.

APOSTROPHE (')
SECTIONS 33, 34, AND 35

The apostrophe shows the possessive form of a noun.

Singular and plural nouns *not* ending in an *s* or *z* sound add an apostrophe and *s* to form the possessive:

a girl's dress, women's magazines

Singular nouns ending in an *s* or *z* sound add an apostrophe and *s* to form the possessive if they are words of one syllable or are stressed on the last syllable:

Keats's poetry, the press's privilege, LaPlace's theory

Plurals ending in an *s* or *z* sound, and singulars *not* stressed on the last syllable, usually add only the apostrophe to form the possessive:

horses' heads, righteousness' sake, Socrates' philosophy, girls' dresses

The apostrophe stands for omitted letters or numerals in contractions:

didn't (did not), rock 'n' roll (rock and roll), would've (would have), '29 (1929)

Be sure the apostrophe stands in the place where the letters or numerals have been left out.

The apostrophe is never used to show plurals of words. Regular plurals should not be confused with *plural possessives*:

PLURAL: horses
PLURAL POSSESSIVE: horses' heads

The apostrophe is used in the formation of plurals only of alphabet letters and numerals:

ABC's, six *e*'s, three 2's

Apostrophes are often omitted from official names or titles:

Teachers College, Womens Rights Organization

BRACKETS ([ ]) SECTION 26

Square brackets are used only to enclose editorial comments, explanations, and corrections in quoted material in order to show that such additions have been inserted by someone else and are not part of the original:

"Phoebe Langworth [Griselda Langworth's elder daughter] was born in Kensington on December 8, 1873, with a cleft palate."

The word *sic* (Latin for *thus*) is inserted in brackets following misspellings or incorrect facts in quoted material in order to show that they are exactly as in the original, and are not quoted in error:

"I was introduced to an interesting young man named Henry Thoro [sic] at Mrs. Emerson's tea."

Brackets are not a substitute for parentheses, and should be used only to indicate editorial insertions.

CAPITALIZATION SECTIONS 40 AND 46

The following rules always apply.
Capitalize the first word of a sentence:

Always capitalize the first word of a sentence.

Capitalize the pronoun *I*.

Capitalize the first word of a full quotation:

> According to Emerson, "A foolish consistency is the hobgoblin of little minds."

Capitalize the first word of every line of poetry written in a traditional form:

> There lies a vale in Ida, lovelier
> Than all the valleys of Ionian hills.

Capitalize the first and last words in a title, and all other words except prepositions and conjunctions (books, plays, motion pictures, poems, essays, stories, articles):

War and Peace
"A Hope to Build On"

Capitalize all proper names — names of persons and pet animals (including nicknames), cities, states, nations, peoples, races, tribes, languages:

Robert F. Kennedy	Ghana
Bobby	Negro
Rover	Iroquois
Minneapolis	Indo-European
Minnesota	Swahili

Capitalize honorary and formal titles when used preceding a proper name:

Senator Long	General Eisenhower
Reverend Mr. Jackson	Mrs. Black
Queen Elizabeth	Dr. Spock
Chief Judge David T. Bazelon	Rabbi David Weiss

Capitalize names or epithets of the Deity:

God	Jehovah
Providence	the Lord

Capitalize trade names:

 Chevrolet   Kodak
 Oxydol   Kleenex

Capitalize names of government agencies and private organizations:

 Federal Bureau of Investigation
 Supreme Court
 Sierra Club
 Daughters of the American Revolution

 The guidelines above always apply. There are some instances, however, in which capitalization varies.

 Capitalize most words derived from proper names:

 Roman candles
 French toast
 Freudian
 Spanish rice
 Englishman

However, exceptions occur frequently:

 venetian blinds
 pasteurization
 guillotine

Verbs derived from proper names are usually not capitalized:

 americanize
 anglicize
 frenchify

Consult a dictionary when you are uncertain about particular cases.

 Do not capitalize honorary or formal titles when they follow a proper name or when they are used in a general sense:

  Elizabeth I, queen of England
  Hugo Black, justice of the Supreme Court

Lyndon B. Johnson was president of the United States.
The governor issued a statement last Wednesday.
We met a prime minister, an archbishop, a senator and a general.

Capitalize points of the compass when they refer to geographic regions, but not when they refer to a direction:

We moved to the Southwest.
We drove southwest for two days
Southern hospitality
southerly winds

Capitalize geographical terms when they are part of a proper name, but not when they are used in a general sense:

Great Plains   plains of Africa
Great Lakes   large lakes
Missouri River   Missouri River valley

Capitalize names of literary periods, important historical events and epochs, but not when used in a general sense:

Middle Ages   medieval
Romantic poets   romantic feeling
World War II   the disastrous war

Generally speaking, capitalize any word which is used as a proper name, or as a part of a proper name, but do not capitalize it in its ordinary sense as a common noun.

Do not capitalize at random for emphasis or simply to show importance.

COLON (:) SECTIONS 24 AND 39

The colon introduces a list of items:

The Declaration of Independence asserts three basic rights: life, liberty, and the pursuit of happiness.

Do not use the colon, however, when such a list functions as the object of a verb or preposition:

The Declaration of Independence asserts our right to life, liberty, and the pursuit of happiness.

Please bring the coffee, sugar, cream, and sweet rolls.

The colon leads up to and introduces a word, a phrase, or a sentence:

The American people crave one thing above all: peace.

The American people crave one thing above all: an end to the war.

The senator argued one main point: The war should be concluded by negotiation rather than by military force.

(Note: Following a colon, the first word of a complete sentence is often capitalized, though it need not be.)

The colon may be used to balance two independent clauses, often for contrast:

You think black: he thinks white.

The colon may follow a date or place name in a diary entry:

December 7, 1941: Today the Japanese attacked Pearl Harbor.

The colon is used after the salutation in business and formal letters:

Dear Sir:

The colon divides a title and subtitle:

The Mirror and the Lamp: Romantic Theory and the Critical Tradition

COMMA (,) SECTIONS 1 THROUGH 20 AND SECTION 37

The comma separates items in a series (Sections 1–6):

Dimes, quarters, and half-dollars are no longer made of pure silver. [*Note*: The comma before *and* may be omitted.]

Do not use a comma to separate only two coordinate items (Section 3):

> Quarters and half-dollars are no longer made of pure silver.

The comma separates two independent sentences when they are joined by a coordinating conjunction (Section 7):

> I did not know what I could do, but I wanted to see what was happening.

Other coordinating conjunctions are and, or, nor, yet. [*Note:* The comma goes *before* the conjunction, not after it.]

Never use a comma to connect two independent sentences without a conjunction. This error is called a "comma splice" (Section 8).

> WRONG: I did not know what I could do, I wanted to see what was happening.

A comma follows an introductory or transitional expression (Section 11):

> In other words, the legality of the claim is still in doubt.
> However, the question must be allowed to rest at this point.

A pair of commas is placed around an introductory or transitional expression when it occurs in midsentence (Section 12):

> The legality of the claim, in other words, is still in doubt.
> The question, however, must be allowed to rest at this point.

Transitional adverbs must not be confused with conjunctions. When joining two sentences with a transitional adverb between them, use a semicolon after the first sentence rather than a comma (Section 13):

WRONG: The house, on the hill, was built in 1824. [Do not put a comma after "house" or "hill" to separate a phrase in normal position from the rest of the sentence.]

2. Joining two independent sentences without a conjunction (see "comma splice" above).

3. Leaving out one of two commas in a pair.

RIGHT: He is, without doubt, the most popular living novelist.

When *two* commas are needed to enclose an expression, be sure to use both. A frequent error is to omit one:

WRONG: He is without doubt, the most popular living novelist.

Any word, phrase, or clause which is either transitional, interruptive, or out of normal order, and occurring in mid-sentence, must be set apart with *two* commas—one at each end.

4. Following a coordinating conjunction.

We tried very hard, but we could not save him. [No comma after "but."]

Long, complicated sentences, particularly those with a lengthy series of items, may have to be rewritten to avoid confusion. Punctuation alone cannot solve all problems of clarity:

POOR: Thus her New England boiled dinner always had, in addition to the corned beef, carrots, beets, boiled potatoes, and cabbage.

REWRITTEN: In addition to the corned beef, her New England dinner always had carrots, beets, boiled potatoes, and cabbage.

(See also Section 6 on using semicolons instead of commas in complicated series.)

The comma also has several arbitrary uses (Section 37). After the salutation in informal letters:

Dear Alex,

Like nonrestrictive clauses, nonrestrictive appositives require commas because they are not essential to distinguish one particular person or thing among others. Commas are NOT used with restrictive appositives.

    His son Bob is a photographer.

"Bob" is an appositive. It distinguishes him from the other sons, and is therefore restrictive. (See Section 18.)

Commas are used with nonrestrictive verbal phrases (Section 19):

    The doe and her fawn, browsing on the fresh sprouts, worked their way along the fence.
    Coming in too low over the hillside, the plane sliced into a clump of trees and crashed.

Commas are NOT used with restrictive verbal phrases:

    The boy eating an ice-cream sandwich is Wesley Johnson's son.
    I saw a man trying to break the lock.

Commas set apart interruptive expressions and sentence modifiers (Section 20):

    You can, no doubt, replace the worn-out parts.
    Some people, unfortunately, do not see a doctor at the first signs of serious illness.
    To tell the truth, we did not expect a favorable response.

The most common errors in using commas:

1. Separating two grammatically related elements that should be kept together.

    WRONG: Playing tennis on Fridays, is her latest habit. [Do not put a comma after "Fridays" to separate subject and verb.]
    WRONG: A tall, slim, girl stood in the doorway. [Do not put a comma after "slim" to separate adjective and noun.]
    WRONG: Quarters, and half-dollars are no longer made of pure silver. [Do not put a comma after "quarters" to separate two coordinate nouns.]

After the complimentary close in all letters:

   Yours truly,
   With love,

Between a name and a degree or honorary title which follows:

   Milton R. Standish, M.D.
   Marguerite Wilson, M.S., F.A.C.P., vice president

Between first and last names when they are reversed:

   Greenfield, William B.
   Arbuckle, Harvey Francis, Jr.
   Hatfield, Conrad, Lt. Gen.

In sentence context, a comma is used in addresses between street, city, state, and country, and after the last item if the sentence continues:

   He presently lives at 1424 West Annandale Blvd., Springfield, Michigan 48511, U.S.A.

   Salinas, California, was then only a sleepy little town.

Place a comma between hundreds, thousands, millions, and so on, in numbers:

   12,308,431

Commas are omitted from computered or machine-handled numbers such as social-security, credit-card, telephone, driver's license, and zip-code numbers, and also from street addresses and page numbers of four digits or more:

   37581 West Mohawk Road
   page 1453

COMPOUND WORDS

   See: Hyphen

DASH (–) SECTIONS 21 AND 23

Like the comma, the dash may be used singly or in pairs. The single dash separates an afterthought, an enlargement, or illustration from the rest of the sentence:

>When the war ended, he took up horse-raising – but that is another story.

The dash often substitutes for a comma, semicolon, or colon in order to suggest the idea of afterthought or enlargement. The dash carries stronger emphasis:

>Carl took three drinks, big ones.
>Carl took three drinks – big ones.
>The American people want one thing above all: peace.
>The American people want one thing above all – peace.
>When the war ended, he took up horse-raising; but that is another story.
>When the war ended, he took up horse-raising – but that is another story.

A *pair* of dashes is used to enclose such material when it is placed in midsentence:

>I have an idea – not an original one, perhaps – for solving the problem.

The single dash is also used in dialogue to indicate interrupted speech:

>"But I didn't even –"

The typewriter keyboard does not have the dash. It is indicated by typing two consecutive hyphens, thus: --

EXCLAMATION POINT (!)

The exclamation point terminates a sentence, like a period. It expresses excitement. Sober-minded teachers and editors warn against it repeatedly as too superficially emotional and melodramatic. But it is unavoidable when violent emotion is called for (Fire! Help!). It is also used to point up humor or irony, or to stress a surprising fact:

> When I turned to the barbecue, Marshall's German shepherd was racing away with something gripped in its teeth — my steak!

The exclamation point can also occur in midsentence with an interruptive expression:

> The "slight increase" in my insurance — two hundred dollars! — was said to be justified by the rising accident rate.

Edgar Allan Poe habitually used exclamation points and italics for heightened emphasis:

> One bound, and I had reached her feet! Shrinking from my touch, she let fall from her head, unloosened, the ghastly cerements which had confined it, and there streamed forth, into the rushing atmosphere of the chamber, huge masses of long and dishevelled hair; *it was blacker than the wings of midnight*!

Present-day writers affect a more coolly sophisticated attitude, and look upon Poe's excitement as naive exaggeration.

HYPHEN (-) SECTIONS 29 THROUGH 32

The hyphen is used when a word must be divided at the end of a line and part of it is carried over to the next line. It is safest to consult a dictionary for proper syllable division, rather than to trust pronunciation.

> EXAMPLES OF SYLLABIFICATION:
> quan-ti-ta-tive
> oc-cur-rence

The following rules always apply:
1. Place the hyphen at the end of the line where the word breaks, never at the beginning of the next.
2. Never hyphenate a word so as to leave standing alone a syllable of only one or two letters (a-bove, love-ly).
3. Never hyphenate a single-syllable word.

4. Never hyphenate numerals or abbreviations.
The hyphen separates individual letters to indicate spelling:

> The prefix of *perspire* is spelled *p-e-r*, not *p-r-e*.

The hyphen has been used to indicate stuttering, usually by poor writers who do not realize it is amateurish and unrealistic:

> "D-d-don't hit me!"

Avoid this sort of thing. (See Section 29.)
The hyphen joins the parts of some compound words:

> baby-sitter
> top-heavy

However, compounds may also appear as two separate words or be written solid as a single word:

> shoulder blade
> bluebird

Compounds will not always be found in a dictionary, but it is worth consulting a good dictionary when in doubt. The trend is toward a preference for either the open or solid form, rather than hyphenation, and some compounds may appear in more than one form. Although no easy rule can be applied, a few common practices may be observed.

Always hyphenate or use the solid form when necessary to distinguish the meaning from words written separately:

> white wash
> whitewash
> slow-moving van
> slow moving-van

Hyphenate compounds in which the two words retain independent meaning:

> nylon-cotton fabric
> red-gold sunset
> husband-wife team

Usually hyphenate compounds derived from noun-verb combinations:

baby-sitter
pumpkin-eater
girl-watcher

Hyphenate phrases used as single words:

an off-the-cuff remark
a down-in-the-mouth expression
a run-of-the-mill specimen

However, do *not* hyphenate phrases when used in normal predicate position:

His remarks were off the cuff.

Hyphenate noun-adverb combinations derived from verbs. But never place a hyphen between a verb and a following adverb:

Don't give us a hand-out.
Scale down the drawings.
Make a scale-down of the drawings.

Note that the *verb*-adverb combinations are never hyphenated. (See Section 30.)

Hyphenate a prefix when the base-word begins with a capital letter:

anti-Nazi
ex-Catholic
pro-American

Hyphenate most prefixes which end in the same letter with which the base word begins:

anti-imperialist
re-entry
co-organizer
EXCEPTIONS: cooperate, preeminent

Hyphenate the prefix *re-* to distinguish meaning from that of a similar word:

recover, re-cover
redress, re-dress
recreation, re-creation

(See Section 31.)

Hyphenate numbers from twenty-one through ninety-nine:

forty-one
forty-first
one hundred forty-one
one thousand six hundred forty-one
twenty-three sixty-fourths

(See Section 32.)

ITALICS (*ITALICS*) SECTIONS 41 AND 47

Indicate italics in manuscript by underlining.
Italics may indicate emphasis. (Remember the example of Poe, however, and use italics sparingly.)

Cheating is the *only* reason for expulsion.

Italics are used for titles of books, plays, motion pictures, long poems, works of art, and periodicals. (Titles of chapters, parts of books, short poems, and short stories are enclosed in quotation marks.)

The Grapes of Wrath
Antony and Cleopatra
Midnight Cowboy
Don Juan
Mona Lisa
Journal of the American Medical Association
"Stopping by Woods on a Snowy Evening"
"Flowering Judas"

Foreign words and phrases are italicized unless they have become absorbed into common English usage:

rapprochement
à la carte

Words referred to as words, and letters as letters, are italicized:

> The word *and* is sometimes omitted from a series of items.
> The letter *e* is the most-used letter in the alphabet.

Names of ships, aircraft, and trains have traditionally been italicized:

> the *Lusitania*
> the *China Clipper*
> the *City of San Francisco*

PARENTHESES ( ) SECTION 22

Parentheses must always come in pairs, never singly. They enclose material which stands outside the sentence pattern, and is read as an "aside":

> Once upon a time (this is an anecdote) I went for a week's holiday on the Continent with an Indian friend.

Any punctuation which belongs with the parenthetical material goes inside the parentheses. Otherwise, all other punctuation marks remain outside:

> The more expensive Persian rugs contain seven or eight hundred knots per square inch (some even have a thousand, although this is unusual).

The period in the preceding example goes outside the parenthesis at the end, because it belongs with the sentence as a whole.

> The more expensive Persian rugs contain seven or eight hundred knots per square inch (some even have a thousand,

although this is unusual), while the cheaper ones are more loosely woven.

The comma goes outside the second parenthesis, because it belongs with the sentence even when the parenthetical material is omitted:

> The more expensive Persian rugs contain seven or eight hundred knots per square inch. (Some even have a thousand, although this is unusual.)

The entire second sentence above is enclosed in parentheses. Therefore, the period goes inside.

PERIOD (.) SECTIONS 25 AND 26

The single period, as everyone knows, marks the end of a sentence. So do the question mark and exclamation point—but they can also be used with interruptive material in midsentence, whereas a period cannot. The single period is the only mark which is used exclusively as a terminal mark and can never be used internally in a sentence.

The period ought to create no problems. However, not everyone is sure exactly where his sentence ends, and sometimes cuts a sentence off too soon, creating an improper fragment:

> The president condemned the student protest movement. Although he should have known better.

The second "sentence" is a subordinate clause, connected to the main sentence by the subordinating conjunction "although." A comma should have been used instead of a period.

Sentence fragments are usually clauses or phrases grammatically related to a main sentence and inadvertently cut off. Ordinarily, a comma or semicolon should replace the incorrect period.

Incomplete sentences are sometimes correct. But they differ importantly from fragments:

You can stay away a long time. Forever, in fact.

The second part is actually not a fragment at all, but rather a condensed or telescoped sentence. Expanded, it would read:

You can stay away forever, in fact.

Such telescoped or abbreviated sentences are quite common in informal writing and in fictional dialogue. They are not amputated fragments belonging with another sentence, but rather independent sentences in their own right, even if incomplete.

POINTS OF ELLIPSIS (...)
SECTIONS 26 AND 43

The ellipsis is indicated by a row of three periods. It represents an omission of words or sentences from quoted material:

"General Custer's attitude on that day, for reasons we can now only conjecture, was apparently moody and withdrawn."

"General Custer's attitude on that day...was apparently moody and withdrawn."

When omitted material comes at the end of a sentence, four periods rather than three are used. Three stand for the omission, while the fourth indicates the end of the sentence:

"General Custer's attitude on that day was apparently moody and withdrawn, although we cannot now offer more than a conjecture as to the reasons."

"General Custer's attitude on that day was apparently moody and withdrawn...."

The ellipsis is often used in imaginative writing to indicate a suspense or lapse of time, or a trailing-off:

"I wonder why...."

Newspaper and magazine columnists frequently separate short comments with ellipsis, especially when many are put together in one paragraph and would otherwise seem run together.

Do not use strings of five or more periods in any situation.

QUESTION MARK (?)
SECTIONS 22 AND 25

The question mark terminates a sentence in the form of a direct question:

What has happened to our liberties?

The question mark may be used internally with an interruptive expression:

The story ends when Goodman Brown returns to the village (or has he actually been dreaming the experience?) and resumes his daily life.

A question may be incorporated into a declarative sentence without quotation marks:

May I ask, What has happened to our liberties?

The question mark is never used when a question is worded indirectly as a declarative statement:

He asked what had happened to our liberties.

QUOTATION MARKS (" ") (' ')
SECTIONS 26, 27, 43, AND 48

Quotation marks are used primarily to enclose words attributed to someone other than the writer.

When complete sentences are quoted, the first word of the quotation is capitalized. A comma or colon is placed just before the first quotation marks:

General MacArthur said, "I shall return."
The regulations state: "Coeds under the age of twenty-one must live in a dormitory."

Fragmentary quotations—a single word or a selected part of a sentence— are *not* capitalized or preceded by a comma or colon. They are worked into the structure of the basic sentence:

> He listed his goal in life as "happiness."
> The witness stated that his attackers were "heavy-set," "unshaven," and "ape-like."

Commas and periods at the end of a quotation always go inside the quotation marks. *Note*: British usage sometimes places them outside, which explains why you may have seen exceptions. But standard American usage *always* places commas and periods inside the second quotation marks, in all situations. Punctuation which precedes the *first* quotation marks, on the other hand, is always outside, because it belongs with the basic sentence.

All punctuation marks other than comma and period go inside final quotation marks if they are part of the quotation, but outside if they are part of the basic sentence:

> He shrieked at his father, "Get off my back!"
> The word he used was "instability"; but I do not think it is accurate.
> She told me I was "too fat"!

In the second example above, a comma would have gone inside the quotation marks, although the semicolon goes outside. In the last example above, a period would have gone inside the quotation marks, although the exclamation point goes outside.

When a full sentence is quoted at the beginning, it is followed by a comma:

> "A foolish consistency is the hobgoblin of little minds," according to Emerson.

When a quoted sentence is interrupted in the middle, the intervening material is set apart with commas:

> "A foolish consistency," according to Emerson, "is the hobgoblin of little minds."

The internal punctuation of a quoted sentence must be preserved as it is in the original. If a quoted sentence is broken at the point where a semicolon or colon occurs, use a comma at the break but shift the semicolon to the end of the inserted material:

> "China will survive her internal upheavals; she always has."
>
> "China will survive her internal upheavals," Harrison claims; "she always has."

Similarly, when two consecutive sentences are quoted with a break between them, the period is placed after the inserted material:

> "We must recognize unpopular governments. They are a part of our world."
>
> "We must recognize unpopular governments," he argued. "They are part of our world."

However, if the quotation ends with a question mark or exclamation point, these marks are retained within the quotation marks:

> "What are your reasons?" he demanded.
> "Get off my back!" his son shrieked.

Single quotation marks (' ') are used to enclose a quotation within a quotation:

> "The witness has used the word 'instability,'" the attorney began.

Note that the comma goes inside *both* sets of quotation marks when they happen to fall together like this.

Quotation marks are sometimes used to enclose a word on a different level of style from that of its context:

> Students are "turned on" by Professor Wainwright's lectures on the impact of the multimedia experience on our culture.

Quotation marks may also be placed around an unfamiliar technical term when it is first used. After it is introduced and explained, the quotation marks are usually dropped:

> These bodies, called "quasars," emit ultraviolet light and radio waves.

Although italics are generally used to indicate a word used as a word, quotation marks may be used instead, particularly if the word has the air of being drawn from some written or spoken context:

> The word "cool" is currently faddish with the under-thirty generation.

Do not try to make a slang term or cliché look better by putting quotation marks around it. Avoid such terms if you are self-conscious about them:

> The character of Ophelia is a "real drag," if I may employ colloquial terminology.

Do not use quotation marks merely as decoration on signs or announcements. Quotation marks are sometimes used to express irony, and decorative marks may inadvertently reverse the meaning. A sign "FRESH" EGGS implies, actually, that the eggs are stale.

SEMICOLON (;)
SECTIONS 6, 9, 10, AND 13

The semicolon has two uses: it connects two independent sentences, and it separates items in a series when commas are not appropriate.

> AS SENTENCE-CONNECTOR: England entered the war in 1914; the United States followed in 1916.

Here the semicolon takes the place of a conjunction or connecting word.

If the second sentence begins with a conjunctive adverb—such as *however, nevertheless,* or *therefore*—be sure to use a semicolon rather than a comma. A comma alone is not used to connect independent sentences:

> England entered the war in 1914; however, the United States did not follow until 1916.

DO NOT use a semicolon to separate a dependent clause or long phrase. A comma should be used instead.

> WRONG: Whitman suddenly developed a highly original style; although he was thirty-six years old and had been a journalist and writer for many years.

Remember: a semicolon connects complete and independent sentences, not the subordinate clauses and phrases *within* a sentence.

The only proper use of a semicolon within a single independent sentence is to separate items in a series when commas might be unclear or too weak.

When a series consists of phrases that have additional commas within them, it is sometimes difficult to recognize the end of each phrase. In such cases, semicolons may be used to mark the larger divisions between items in the series, while commas mark the smaller divisions within the phrases:

> At different times and places it may be a circular disk like a saucer, often with a small protrusion in the center like a knob on a teakettle lid; elliptical or bean-shaped like a flattened sphere; a circular base supporting a dome-like superstructure; a sphere surrounded by a central platform, like Saturn in its rings; long and thin like a cigar; a tapered sphere like a teardrop; spindle-shaped, with or without knobs on the ends; or a double- or triple-decked form like a stack of plates.